WITHDRAWN
from MSU-WP Garn

D0559202

PN   78532
710   Mudrick, Marvin.
.M76   The man in the
        machine

DATE			
APR 2 4 1990			

© THE BAKER & TAYLOR CO.

THE
MAN
IN
THE
MACHINE

THE
MAN
IN
THE
MACHINE

Marvin Mudrick

 HORIZON PRESS   New York

Copyright © 1977 by Marvin Mudrick

Library of Congress Cataloging in Publication Data

Mudrick, Marvin.
  The man in the machine.

  1. Literature, Modern—History and criticism
—Addresses, essays, lectures. I. Title.
PN710.M76   809'.03   75-5994
ISBN 0-8180-1164-5

Manufactured in the United States of America

To Al Stephens

Contents

The Man
in the Machine

Poe the demon mystery-solver once "proved" that a purported chess-playing machine had a man in it all the time. However, scholars *proved* later that Poe had cribbed the entire proof; but he was just showing off, since left to his own devices he always gave machines the benefit of the doubt. Poe believed deep down (1) that machines should be left to their own devices, and (2) that the man in the machine was absurd and excessive, because how could the contained be a bigger mystery than the container? Poe really did prefer machines to people, he liked mysteries with blueprints and clockwork innards, mechanical monsters in verse and prose. He fascinated Baudelaire and Mallarmé by making mysteries seem formal, logical, and literary; and they paid him back by reintroducing him into Anglo-American literature under the solemn auspices of modernism. (They couldn't have guessed that in English, try as he might to scare the hell out of us, he was very funny. If Poe himself had guessed how funny he was, he might have been the W. C. Fields of literature: dauntless, morose, uneasy, oozing the undulant lingo of the village mountebank, donning a pair of scuffed kid gloves with the ends of the fingers worn through, delicately sipping redeye in the frontier saloon, ogling the ladies in wild surmise, that gravied vest! those shifty eyes!) Poe lives. Absurd and excessive, a bigger mystery than any of the books which contain him, American rankness with a little French dressing, he had the effrontery to palm off on us the silliest, least interesting, and most influential of twentieth-century critical dogmas: that books are machines with nobody inside.

1.
Looking for Kellermann

There is an early scene in *The Metamorphosis* as comical and heartbreaking as any in fiction. Gregor Samsa, having awakened one morning to find himself "transformed in his bed into a gigantic insect," tries to be reasonable about the event (doubtless it's only nerves), tries to think his way through it or around it, tries to take his mind off it by recollecting his ineffectual life, but it persists ("It was no dream"); he won't of course come out of his room or let anybody in; his parents and sister are alarmed; he will be late for work; the chief clerk arrives from the office to investigate his tardiness; still he delays, trying with his altered voice to placate and reassure them (but " 'That was no human voice,' said the chief clerk"); and at last, edging his unfamiliar bulk out into the room where the others are waiting, he presents them with the shape and size of the problem:

> . . . he heard the chief clerk utter a loud "Oh!"—it sounded like a gust of wind—and now he could see the man, standing as he was nearest to the door, clapping one hand before his open mouth and slowly backing away as if driven by some invisible steady pressure. . . .

Gregor knows it's now or never:

> ". . . Where are you going, sir? To the office? Yes? Will you give a true account of all this? One can be temporarily incapaci-

11

tated, but that's just the moment for remembering former services and bearing in mind that later on, when the incapacity has been got over, one will certainly work with all the more industry and concentration. I'm loyally bound to serve the chief, you know that very well. Besides, I have to provide for my parents and my sister. I'm in great difficulties, but I'll get out of them again. . . ."

He fails, however, to make the intended impression:

". . . Sir, sir, don't go away without a word to me to show that you think me in the right at least to some extent!"

But at Gregor's very first words the chief clerk had already backed away and only stared at him with parted lips over one twitching shoulder. And while Gregor was speaking he did not stand still one moment but stole away towards the door, without taking his eyes off Gregor, yet only an inch at a time, as if obeying some secret injunction to leave the room. He was already at the hall, and the suddenness with which he took his last step out of the living room would have made one believe he had burned the sole of his foot. Once in the hall he stretched his right arm before him towards the staircase, as if some supernatural power were waiting there to deliver him.

Gregor perceived that the chief clerk must on no account be allowed to go away in this frame of mind if his position in the firm were not to be endangered to the utmost. . . .

Gregor therefore attempts a decisive movement, which temporarily galvanizes his petrified mother into upsetting the coffee pot:

The chief clerk, for the moment, had quite slipped from . . . [Gregor's] mind; instead, he could not resist snapping his jaws together at the sight of the streaming coffee. That made his mother scream again, she fled from the table and fell into the arms of his father, who hastened to catch her. But Gregor had now no time to spare for his parents; the chief clerk was already on the stairs; with his chin on the banisters he was taking one last backward look. Gregor made a spring, to be as sure as possible of overtaking him; the chief clerk must have divined his intention, for he leaped down several steps and vanished; he was still yelling "Ugh!" and it echoed through the whole staircase.

Nothing remains but for Gregor's father, "hissing and crying 'Shoo!' like a savage," to drive him back into his room and slam the door shut behind him.

Terms like "allegory," "symbol," "ambiguity" will carry a Kafka critic through the scene, but they won't give him the feel of it. "It was no dream," says Kafka, tactfully warning us to pay attention. Gregor is an unallegorical king-size bug with problems. The chief clerk is a man in a funk. Their encounter, which is funny but not profound, opposes a resistible force with a movable object, and doesn't teach us anything except how not to behave in emergencies.

Besides, the chief clerk is busier than his function warrants. He does something like a vaudeville routine, straight man turned top banana, profiting by an unforeseen opportunity. The comic focus here isn't Gregor, it's the chief clerk: in the course of the scene Gregor's plight gracefully dwindles into a sufficient pretext for the chief clerk's consternation, which (stunning invention) Kafka savors and indulges. The scene might have been very different, terse, more solicitous of Gregor and the plot, without such lingering emphasis on the chief clerk's pop-eyed suspension of disbelief as, staring and staring, he backpedals with tremendous slowness to the point from which, at length, he will be capable of breaking the spell and hurling himself down the stairs to freedom. The chief clerk, if he hadn't delighted Kafka, might have been all function. How will the world, not merely Gregor's family, react to Gregor's new condition? The chief clerk could show us. In fact he does show us, so amply that what he shows becomes less noteworthy than what he is: not a meaning but a presence.

Life, springing up like mushrooms, is Kafka's subject, what he looks for whenever he isn't at the mercy of his despondency. Here are two pieces of evidence from his diaries. In an entry of 1911—*The Metamorphosis* was written in 1913— he described, without yet recognizing what it was, the stony ground out of which the story would grow:

> February 19. When I wanted to get out of bed this morning I simply folded up. This has a very simple cause. I am completely overworked. Not by my office but my other work. The office

has an innocent share in it only to the extent that, if I did not have to go there, I could live calmly for my own work and should not have to waste these six hours a day which have tormented me to a degree that you cannot imagine, especially on Friday and Saturday, because I was full of my own things. In the final analysis, I know, that is just talk, the fault is mine and the office has a right to make the most definite and justified demands on me. But for me in particular it is a horrible double life from which there is probably no escape but insanity. . . .

In the other diary entry, the manifestation Kafka always looks for is already so nearly explicit in the congenial circumstances that he can discover and describe it at once:

November 27[, 1910]. Bernhard Kellermann read aloud. "Some unpublished things from my pen," he began. Apparently a kind person, an almost gray brush of hair, painstakingly close-shaven, a sharp nose, the flesh over his cheekbones often ebbs and flows like a wave. He is a mediocre writer with good passages (a man goes out into the corridor, coughs and looks around to see if anyone is there), also an honest man who wants to read what he promised, but the audience wouldn't let him; because of the fright caused by the first story about a hospital for mental disorders, because of the boring manner of the reading, the people, despite the story's cheap suspense, kept leaving one by one with as much zeal as if someone were reading next door. When, after the first third of the story, he drank a little mineral water, a whole crowd of people left. He was frightened. "It is almost finished," he lied outright. When he was finished everyone stood up, there was some applause that sounded as though there were one person in the midst of all the people standing up who had remained seated and was clapping by himself. But Kellermann still wanted to read on, another story, perhaps even several. But all he could do against the departing tide was to open his mouth. Finally, after he had taken counsel, he said, "I should still like very much to read a little tale that will take only fifteen minutes. I will pause for five minutes." Several still remained, whereupon he read a tale containing passages that were justification for anyone to run out from the farthest point of the hall right through the middle of and over the whole audience.

These things happen, and there is no help for them. The chief clerk, quite beside himself (nobody else to turn to, no salvation anywhere), spontaneously invents an attitude of prayer: "he stretched his right arm before him towards the staircase, as if some supernatural power were waiting there to deliver him." Kellermann, frightened and irrepressible, exercises his will against an audience that does its magical disappearing act in bursts of cold energy. These things are perfectly straightforward and clear. The chief clerk and Kellermann are as real as mushrooms, they cannot be said to "stand for" anything else since they never cease to be only themselves, they are too dense to dissipate themselves.[1] At the instant when Kafka notices them, circumstances have braced them into self-definition, toward the accomplishing of which the circumstances (the story, the plot, the situation, the moral, the theme) are merely necessary machinery.

The chief clerk and Kellermann are pure and intense instances of life in print. Life isn't always easy to recognize in print, it may be diffused over many pages of incident and contingency, it may go by in a phrase or a barely perceptible turn of events while the reader's attention wanders, it may too quickly get lost or mangled in the machinery; but the reader of fiction has no alternative to looking for it, since everything else is already laid out in Northrop Frye's elegant Linnaean categories, or Wayne Booth's conventional morality disguised as an inventory of handy devices, or Ian Watt's sociology, or Albert Guerard's Jungian recipes, or R. S. Crane's infatuation with thoroughly lubricated plots, or F. R. Leavis's rack-and-thumbscrew culture-obsession. Looking for Kellermann, the reader isn't employing a critical procedure, rather he's manifesting a human quality—companionableness, perhaps. Nor is this quality biased in the direction of so idiosyncratic a writer as Kafka (who anyhow is far more likely to be admired for his

---

[1] Like those enigmas of astronomy, "the 'black holes' predicted by the general theory of relativity: objects so compact that even light cannot escape their gravitational pull." Melvin A. Ruderman, "Solid Stars," *Scientific American*, 224, No. 2 (Feb. 1971), 24.

private machinery of mystification and self-pity, out of which he was only occasionally able to dislodge such Mozartian farce as the early pages of *The Metamorphosis*). Indeed, the quality is probably more often prompted and gratified by the novels of so evidently conventional a novelist as Trollope.

Critics have had a hard time with Trollope. He won't sit still for a portrait[2] (sometimes he looks like minor-league Austen, sometimes like an unflashy and tough-minded Thackeray, sometimes like a cigars-and-whiskey George Eliot); he is obviously an intelligent and talented writer who merits examination; having published more than fifty books, he must have written well in some and ill in others, and—worse luck—even critics have to read a fair number of them before venturing to make distinctions.

Yet Trollope is an astonishingly consistent writer, who gave the Victorian lending-library subscribers exactly their money's worth with almost every installment. According to Trollope his secret, which he revealed (posthumously!) in his *Autobiography*, was that he had succeeded in his conscious aim of turning novel-writing into an honest and well-paid craft of this many hours and that many words per day:

> Every word of . . . [*Lady Anna*] was written at sea, during the two months required for our voyage, and was done day by day —with the intermission of one day's illness—for eight weeks, at the rate of 66 pages of manuscript in each week, every page of manuscript containing 250 words. Every word was counted. I have seen work come back to an author from the press with terrible deficiencies as to the amount supplied. Thirty-two pages have perhaps been wanted for a number, and the printers with all their art could not stretch the matter to more than twenty-eight or -nine! The work of filling up must be very dreadful. I have sometimes been ridiculed for the methodical details of my business. But by these contrivances I have been preserved from many troubles; and I have saved others with whom I have worked—editors, publishers, and printers—from much trouble also.

---

[2]At which I make an attempt in Chapter V.

(*Lady Anna*, by the way, is a solid and convincing novel.) Actually, Trollope had found out how to do most efficiently what he would likely have done if penury had obliged him to scribble day and night in an attic on a diet of bread and water. He was by temperament and talent a journeyman novelist (the term doesn't mean "bad novelist"), he was deliberate rather than mechanical, and his novels are models of immediate unmeretricious attractiveness, credible intrigue, momentum, suspense, breadth of knowledge about social and personal relations, satisfying disentanglement and resolution. He hasn't much gift for long or climactic scenes; he would rather ruminate and sum up than dramatize; he doesn't do low or rural characters well, and he often does them at immoderate length; he tends, especially when he grows anxious about the reader's memory of previous installments, to be prolix and repetitive (and even for so unprecedented a manufacturer of words "the work of filling up" two or three triple-decker novels per year may now and then have been, if not "very dreadful," at least troublesome). But his shortcomings are as evident in the novel Trollopians consider his masterpiece, *The Way We Live Now*, as in any they consider weak and mediocre, in which moreover most of Trollope's skills are as evident as they are in *The Way We Live Now*. Surely no novelist would seem less likely to suggest the obtrusiveness and uncontrollability of human nature.

The obvious anomaly among Trollope's novels is *Barchester Towers*. It's the only Victorian comedy of manners that can be mentioned with *Pride and Prejudice* or *Emma*. Only in *Barchester Towers* does Trollope allow his characters the scope of unsuperintended talk and activity with which they can begin to assert their full claim on us and on one another (by comparison, *The Way We Live Now* is watchful and mature); the most audacious claim, the Signora Neroni's to be all at the same time mysteriously and perhaps hideously crippled, beautiful and clever, irresistible and immune, a comic and slightly sinister apparition of uninhibited will as she rides like the wind into Mrs. Proudie's reception:

> At last a carriage dashed up to the hall steps with a very different manner of approach from that of any other vehicle

that had been there that evening. A perfect commotion took place. The doctor, who heard it as he was standing in the drawing-room, knew that his daughter was coming, and retired into the furthest corner, where he might not see her entrance. Mrs. Proudie perked herself up, feeling that some important piece of business was in hand. . . .

The Signora having arrived, "Mr. Slope hurried into the hall to give his assistance":

> He was, however, nearly knocked down and trampled on by the cortège that he encountered on the hall steps. He got himself picked up as well as he could, and followed the cortège up stairs. The signora was carried head foremost, her head being the care of her brother and an Italian man-servant who was accustomed to the work; her feet were in the care of the lady's maid and the lady's Italian page; and Charlotte Stanhope followed to see that all was done with due grace and decorum. In this manner they climbed easily into the drawing-room, and a broad way through the crowd having been opened, the signora rested safely on her couch. She had sent a servant beforehand to learn whether it was a right or a left hand sofa, for it required that she should dress accordingly, particularly as regarded her bracelets.

Thereupon Trollope settles down next to the lady and for a full paragraph indulges himself and us in a wistful feast of appreciation:

> And very becoming her dress was. It was white velvet, without any other garniture than rich white lace worked with pearls across her bosom, and the same round the armlets of her dress. Across her brow she wore a band of red velvet, on the centre of which shone a magnificent Cupid in mosaic, the tints of whose wings were of the most lovely azure, and the colour of his chubby cheeks the clearest pink. On the one arm which her position required her to expose she wore three magnificent bracelets, each of different stones. Beneath her on the sofa, and over the cushion and head of it, was spread a crimson silk mantle or shawl, which went under her whole body and concealed her feet. Dressed as she was and looking as she did, so beautiful and yet so motionless, with the pure brilliancy of her white dress brought out and strengthened by the colour beneath it, with that

lovely head, and those large bold bright staring eyes, it was impossible that either man or woman should do other than look at
her.

Projectile, serpent (lamia), *femme fatale*, splendid in the "grace
and decorum" with which she and her attendants "climb easily" over any intermediate bodies, an unaccommodated presence coming into focus in electric repose as Venus among the
barbarians, she is more than a match for that Gorgon of the
diocese, Mrs. Proudie, who can't refrain—denouncing the susceptible Mr. Slope—from invoking demonology to explain the
Signora's magnetism:

> ". . . Do you think I have not heard of your kneelings at that
> creature's feet—that is if she has any feet—and of your constant
> slobbering over her hand? . . ."

Trollope never does so well with anybody else, not even
elsewhere in *Barchester Towers* (though Bertie Stanhope, the
Signora's brother, is almost as overpowering in his casual in-
discretions to the Bishop at the same reception), not even elsewhere with the Signora herself, with whom in a provincial Victorian setting he can do little, after all, except find a
sentimental function for her in the plot.

Customarily, Trollope is too prudent to be tempted by
phenomena that threaten to exceed the requirements of his
plots. If he weren't also a passionate man, there wouldn't be
much else to say about the mass of his work. He prides himself
on being a craftsman, what he aims at is fitness, but he is a
passionate man: his job as he sees it is to keep things under
control, but he starts with the handicap of having a great deal
to control. Some of the fun of reading him is in looking for
moods that don't fit, feelings that get rather out of hand, surprises. For instance, he is the only Victorian novelist who gives
the impression that men and women sometimes touch each
other for purposes neither celestial nor infernal but simply because they like to. To be a Victorian novelist, however, is not
to be in a position to take exuberant advantage of this insight,
which makes itself felt as more than an ultrasonic vibration
only in the guise of Trollope's knowledgeable gallantry toward

his female characters, or, more eccentrically, in his fixed conviction about the way in which women fall in love.

Trollope believes that a woman falls in love just once, perhaps on the most accidental provocation with the most trivial man, but that, once she has given her heart (Trollope's locution), she is helpless to change; no other man on earth has a chance, lovable and excellent though he may be, to rouse her (and Trollope has a very specific sense of what *that* means). The conviction tinges with oddness many otherwise impeccably serviceable plots (including the plot of *The Way We Live Now*), but in one instance drives Trollope into putting together a plot that might fairly be called Sophoclean in its arterial connections with the feelings of the characters. *The Vicar of Bullhampton* opens as an idyll about the likable and happily married young vicar and his wife, who with the best and most auspicious intentions try to arrange a marriage between his best friend, the squire, and her best friend, an attractive young woman who happens to be visiting them. But, as the vicar and his wife don't know, the wife's friend has already "given her heart" elsewhere. The consequences, in the gradually darkening landscape of the novel, are immitigable misery for the squire, a loosing of old ties between all of them, and something like an awakening out of Eden for the vicar and his wife. Trollope's own strong nature, which ordinarily he represses for the sake of his plots, takes its revenge on this particular plot by reminding itself of a previous commitment. For once in Trollope, action is nothing and fate is everything. In *Barchester Towers* (as in *The Metamorphosis*), the characters are all large and free enough to direct and dominate the plot without destroying it; in most of Trollope's other novels, the characters more or less discreetly subordinate themselves to the plot. But in *The Vicar of Bullhampton* (as, with due regard for differences of scale and power, in *Oedipus Rex*), there are no characters and the plot has already happened: Trollope's—or the gods'—fixation has decided the issue; the wife's friend is the doomed and necessary instrument of fatal passion, which paralyzes all the characters and precedes and nullifies the plot. Trollope himself is the hero, and passion is the plot.

Of course the novel everybody praises for its plot is *Tom Jones*. "Upon my word," exclaimed Coleridge, confounding English music-boxes with Greek violins, "I think the Oedipus Tyrannus, The Alchemist, and Tom Jones, the three most perfect plots ever planned." In "The Concept of Plot and the Plot of *Tom Jones*," R. S. Crane cites Coleridge as well as other enthusiasts, and attempts with a few neo-Aristotelian flourishes to rationalize what everybody sees in all that whizzing and whirring machinery. Crane's (and Fielding's) euphemism for the machinery, whenever its motions more than usually deny the likelihood of will and reason in human events, is "Fortune"; but just once Fielding manages a shocking and authoritative intervention into a character's most intimate concerns by Fortune herself. It occurs in the scene in which Captain Blifil, at the summit of his influence, swelling with mischief, scheming and scheming, plainly the capital villain with a voluptuous career ahead of him in the remaining nine-tenths of the novel, suffers a brusque and unanticipated reverse:

> But while the captain was one day busied in deep contemplations of this kind . . . just at the very instant when his heart was exulting in meditations on the happiness which would accrue to him by Mr. Allworthy's death, he himself—died of an apoplexy.

A novelist who can afford to cut off the villain in his prime is being altogether serious about the terrible chanciness of life. For a moment in the novel, Fortune isn't a label or an excuse but the goddess incarnate.

Aside from this apotheosis, however, the plot of *Tom Jones* is machinery, and the characters are the ignoble functions that the plot deserves. One critic Crane fails to cite is Dr. Johnson, who, comparing Fielding's characters with Richardson's, remarked that "Characters of manners are very entertaining; but they are to be understood by a more superficial observer than characters of nature, where a man must dive into the recesses of the human heart"; and Johnson "used to quote with approbation a saying of Richardson's, 'that the virtues of Fielding's heroes were the vices of a truly good man.' " Fanciers of carefree and undiscriminating coitus rise in a body to defend Fielding and Tom himself against this last, presumably puritanical indictment; but the indictment is elastic enough to comprehend, besides the censure of Tom's philandering, a more general censure of the characters of the novel. "Good" and "bad" alike, not only do they lack principle, they aren't—in spite of accepted critical opinion—typically subject to impulse, sexual or other; on the contrary, they are as unimpulsive and opportunistic as the plot.[3] Henry Fielding, justice of the peace for the district of Westminster, tends to regard the human heart as typically a cloaca of mean calculations which, if they didn't for the most part cancel one another out, would make the world as uninterruptedly disagreeable as it must often seem during the proceedings of a petty law-court:

Mrs. Honour had scarce sooner parted from her young lady, than something (for I would not, like the old woman in Quevedo, injure the devil by any false accusation, and possibly he might have no hand in it)—but something, I say, suggested itself to her, that by sacrificing Sophia and all her secrets to Mr. Western, she might probably make her fortune. Many considerations urged this discovery. The fair prospect of a handsome reward for so great and acceptable a service to the squire tempted her avarice; and again, the danger of the enterprise she had undertaken; the uncertainty of its success; night, cold, robbers, ravishers, all alarmed her fears. So forcibly did all these operate upon her, that she was almost determined to go directly to the squire, and to lay open the whole affair. She was, however, too upright a judge to decree on one side before she had heard the other. And here, first, a journey to London appeared very strongly in support of Sophia. She eagerly longed to see a place in which she fancied charms short only of those which a raptured saint imagines in heaven. In the next place, as she knew Sophia to have much more generosity than her master, so her

---

[3]*Joseph Andrews* is a better novel because (1) in it Fielding, having undertaken the obligations of parody, is content to work on a smaller scale, toward comic effects that are relatively unforced and good-humored; and (2) the fact that the target of the parody is *Pamela* requires Fielding to keep his hero chaste no matter what, and so provides a (parasitic and burlesque) internal tension which is Fielding's most plausible approximation of a moral order.

fidelity promised her a greater reward than she could gain by treachery. She then cross-examined all the articles which had raised her fears on the other side, and found, on fairly sifting the matter, that there was very little in them. . . .

Page after page is expended on such arithmetic, the incantatory recitation of which Fielding's admirers are pleased to consider a comic, because fearlessly realistic, exposure of motives. As for the motive of common decency, the author of *Tom Jones*—benevolent and spacious survey of mankind—seems in his researches to have missed it entirely, or to have confused it (as in Allworthy) with complacent brainlessness. In this world of moral defectives, the only cure for Mrs. Honour's calculation is Tom's "impulse" to commit carefree and undiscriminating coitus. Or as Crane says, finding mankind as little to his taste as Fielding does, Tom is "a young man whose lack of security and imprudence more than offset his natural goodness, living in a world in which the majority of people are ill-natured and selfish." How glum, and what a squinty perch of condescension from which to take the measure of the rest of us.

But most of us don't appear at our best in a courtroom. Kafka's Kellermann is feeble, crafty, dauntless (like his American cousins, E.A. Poe and W.C. Fields), as full of incommunicable truths as any incompetent writer or living soul; but, observed from the professional height at which Fielding exerts his vested authority, he would only resemble every other prisoner at the bar. Fielding himself is Tolstoy's judge Ivan Ilych, or "the celebrated doctor" to whom the judge is compelled, in his mortal extremity as a poor forked animal, to bring his appeal:

> It was not a question of Ivan Ilych's life or death, but one between a floating kidney and appendicitis. And that question the doctor solved brilliantly, as it seemed to Ivan Ilych, in favour of the appendix, with the reservation that should an examination of the urine give fresh indications the matter would be reconsidered. All this was just what Ivan Ilych had himself brilliantly accomplished a thousand times in dealing with men on trial. The doctor summed up just as brilliantly, looking over his spectacles triumphantly and even gaily at the accused. From the

SMS UNIVERSITY
WEST PLAINS BRANCH

78532

doctor's summing up Ivan Ilych concluded that things were bad, but that for the doctor, and perhaps for everybody else, it was a matter of indifference, though for him it was bad. And this conclusion struck him painfully, arousing in him a great feeling of pity for himself and of bitterness towards the doctor's indifference to a matter of such importance.

Tolstoy shows here how Fielding, confronted by Fielding, might be metamorphosed into Kellermann; he even shows how such an unimaginable Fielding might become attuned to a voice of conscience that begins to sound, hair-raisingly, like the voice of God:

> The pain again grew more acute, but he did not stir and did not call. He said to himself: "Go on! Strike me! But what is it for? What have I done to Thee? What is it for?"
>
> Then he grew quiet and not only ceased weeping but even held his breath and became all attention. It was as though he were listening not to an audible voice but to the voice of his soul, to the current of thoughts arising within him.
>
> "What is it you want?" was the first clear conception capable of expression in words, that he heard. . . .

The only novelist writing in English who has a comparable didactic boldness is D. H. Lawrence.[4] In the 'thirties it was fashionable to dismiss Lawrence for this preoccupation with matters of life and death; in the 'seventies it's becoming feasible to explain why, "a tubercular plebeian cuckold married to a healthy aristocrat," he went as wrong as he did.[5] But the case of Lawrence the valetudinarian lowbrow needn't detain us because, all by himself, Lawrence the journeyman novelist is a

---

[4]Of whom much more in Chapter II.

[5]The reason, we now learn, was his morbid attitude toward women. As "Briefly Noted" (the anonymous reviewer) of *The New Yorker* noted briefly in a review of Kate Millett's *Sexual Politics* (September 19, 1970, p. 137): "Miss Millett proves men's wickedness mainly from the work of several writers who are contemptuous of or hostile toward women. She is an acute literary analyst. Unfortunately for her argument, though, the authors she has chosen are in such psychological trouble themselves that it is hard to agree that they express typical attitudes toward women. Ruskin, for example, was impotent. D. H. Lawrence, a tubercular plebeian cuckold married to a healthy aristocrat, evidently had to assert his dominance in fantasies on

maker of moments and episodes that pass the Kellermann test and that oughtn't to offend the healthiest aristocrat.

An instance is Chapter XIV ("Water-Party") of *Women in Love*. It has very little polemic, it's mostly action: feelings, meetings, transformations. The four principal characters converge into it with their powerfully conflicting demands, and arrive at the end of it committed to the current of mingled purposes that will carry them together all the way into one sort of exile or another, one sort of consummation or another. The symmetry of the chapter has the look of Fate, but Fate as choice—not what is done to them (by the gods or an obsessed author or by Captain Blifil's Fortune) but what they grandly and easily do to themselves; thus they can just as easily, before they choose, pause in a timeless place to take their pleasure:

> The sisters found a little place where a tiny stream flowed into the lake, with reeds and flowery marsh of pink willow herb, and a gravelly bank to the side. Here they ran delicately ashore, with their frail boat, the two girls took off their shoes and stockings and went through the water's edge to the grass. The tiny ripples of the lake were warm and clear, they lifted their boat on to the bank, and looked round with joy. They were quite alone in a forsaken little stream-mouth, and on the knoll just behind was the clump of trees.
>
> "We will bathe just for a moment," said Ursula, "and then we'll have tea."

So they bathe, and "when they had run and danced themselves dry, the girls . . . sat down to the . . . tea," which

> . . . was hot and aromatic, there were delicious little sandwiches of cucumber and of caviare, and winy cakes.
>
> "Are you happy, Prune?" cried Ursula in delight, looking at her sister.

---

paper, but few men have been so overmatched in marriage. *Et ainsi de suite.* Most of Miss Millett's masculine theorists writing about women are the sexual equivalent of Hitler writing on government: striking, unsound, and out of the main line of cultural evolution." On the evidence of this review, "Briefly Noted" is a ninety-proof main-lining swinger of either sex, rather like Tom Jones of the novel or the movie or the TV-*cum*-Las Vegas scene. *Und so weiter.*

"Ursula, I'm perfectly happy," replied Gudrun gravely, looking at the westering sun.

When Gerald "rescues" Gudrun from the wild cattle, she is brought back with a bump to time and love and other daily threats:

"You think I'm afraid of you and your cattle, don't you?" she asked.

His eyes narrowed dangerously. There was a faint domineering smile on his face.

"Why should I think that?" he said.

She was watching him all the time with her dark, dilated, inchoate eyes. She leaned forward and swung round her arm, catching him a light blow on the face with the back of her hand.

"That's why," she said, mocking.

And she felt in her soul an unconquerable desire for deep violence against him. She shut off the fear and dismay that filled her conscious mind. She wanted to do as she did, she was not going to be afraid.

He recoiled from the slight blow on his face. He became deadly pale, and a dangerous flame darkened his eyes. For some seconds he could not speak, his lungs were so suffused with blood, his heart stretched almost to bursting with a great gush of ungovernable emotion. It was as if some reservoir of black emotion had burst within him, and swamped him.

"You have struck the first blow," he said at last, forcing the words from his lungs, in a voice so soft and low, it sounded like a dream within her, not spoken in the outer air.

"And I shall strike the last," she retorted involuntarily, with confident assurance. He was silent, he did not contradict her.

Gudrun determines their fate and then prophesies it: transitory words as she speaks them turn to stone; prophecy is like symbolism, it sacrifices the fact to the meaning. Gudrun has already forgotten what she discovered with Ursula by their little stream away from the hubbub of the festival—that the living make no sacrifices, that they give up nothing, have their cake and eat it too. But timeless dallying by a stream is easier on the nerves than the mere daily facts of life. Gudrun, uncomfortable with mere facts, stares them to stone: for Gudrun and Gerald, the festival that ends in death by water must be portentous and symbolic (whereas for the other pair of lovers, readier to take facts as they come, it's an eventful party that ends very badly).

What Gudrun discovers once and forgets quickly in *Women in Love*, Walter Morel in *Sons and Lovers* exemplifies unthinkingly every morning of his life. Lawrence, lapsing for a moment from the parricidal vindictiveness with which elsewhere in his autobiographical novel he pursues his father's ghost, shows us in a single passage not what the elder Morel is *like* (wretched husband and father, clod, boor, drunken brute) but what to himself, out of the world's eye, he always and adequately *is*:

> He always made his own breakfast. Being a man who rose early and had plenty of time he did not, as some miners do, drag his wife out of bed at six o'clock. At five, sometimes earlier, he woke, got straight out of bed, and went downstairs. When she could not sleep, his wife lay waiting for this time, as for a period of peace. The only real rest seemed to be when he was out of the house.
>
> He went downstairs in his shirt and then struggled into his pit-trousers, which were left on the hearth to warm all night. There was always a fire, because Mrs. Morel raked. And the first sound in the house was the bang, bang of the poker against the raker, as Morel smashed the remainder of the coal to make the kettle, which was filled and left on the hob, finally boil. His cup and knife and fork, all he wanted except just the food, was laid ready on the table on a newspaper. Then he got his breakfast, made the tea, packed the bottom of the doors with rugs to shut out the draught, piled a big fire, and sat down to an hour of joy. He toasted his bacon on a fork and caught the drops of fat on his bread; then he put the rasher on his thick slice of bread, and cut off chunks with a clasp-knife, poured his tea into his saucer, and was happy. . . .

Life is the pleasure of one's company, the pleasure of routine and need. Symbols, whatever they point to and stand for, suggest that life is breaking down and coming apart. Life undivided is the density of particulars, of things and persons:

> . . . he went upstairs to his wife with a cup of tea because she was ill, and because it occurred to him.

"I've brought thee a cup o' tea, lass," he said.

"Well, you needn't, for you know I don't like it," she replied.

"Drink it up; it'll pop thee off to sleep again."

She accepted the tea. It pleased him to see her take it and sip it.

"I'll back my life there's no sugar in," she said.

"Yi—there's one big 'un," he replied, injured.

"It's a wonder," she said, sipping again.

She had a winsome face when her hair was loose. He loved her to grumble at him in this manner. He looked at her again, and went, without any sort of leave-taking. He never took more than two slices of bread and butter to eat in the pit, so an apple or an orange was a treat to him. He always liked it when she put one out for him. He tied a scarf round his neck, put on his great, heavy boots, his coat, with the big pocket, that carried his snap-bag and his bottle of tea, and went forth into the fresh morning air, closing, without locking, the door behind him. He loved the early morning, and the walk across the fields. So he appeared at the pit-top, often with a stalk from the hedge between his teeth, which he chewed all day to keep his mouth moist, down the mine, feeling quite as happy as when he was in the field.

In *War and Peace*, the prisoners who are about to be shot "could not believe it because they alone knew what their life meant to them, and so they neither understood nor believed that it could be taken from them." Mortal and incommunicable flesh and blood, "they alone knew": but Tolstoy knows, and makes us know too. Gudrun alone knows, refusing to be known, what it is to tear herself from Gudrun loving to Gudrun hateful; Morel alone knows on his pulse the blessedness of the morning; Captain Blifil alone knows, an instant before he is struck down, the inextinguishable satisfactions of villainy. And the omniscient author (not at all in the sense of a handy device for expert novelists) knows, though it's just as well that the character doesn't know that the author knows: imagine poor Kellermann seeing Kafka in the audience and knowing—through some diabolical dispensation—what it is to be Franz Kafka sitting out there observing Bernhard Kellermann in the very act of making an immortal ass of himself. Thank God for privacy, or the delusion of it.

Life, private or not, is always excessive and singular (but a machine is an allegory, functional and full of resonances), life is Trollope's obsession about women in love, or Chaucer's fascination with the excessive and singular phenomenon of flesh and blood in a prodigious sweat:

> His hakeney, that was al pomely grys,
> So swatte that it wonder was to see;
> It semed as he had priked miles three.
> The hors eek that his yeman rood upon
> So swatte that unnethe myght it gon.
> About the peytrel stood the foom ful hye;
> He was of foom al flekked as a pye. . . .
> He hadde ay priked lik as he were wood.
> A clote-leef he hadde under his hood
> For swoot, and for to keep his heed from heete.
> But it was joye for to seen hym swete!
> His forheed dropped as a stillatorie. . . .[6]

(This is the Canon suddenly arriving among the Canterbury pilgrims.) "But it was joye for to seen hym swete!": life delighting in life, God delighting in Creation. Chaucer sees things this way all the time.

The least allegorical, and therefore the most novelistic, of long works of fiction is Chaucer's *Troilus and Criseyde*. It is continuously intense, energetic, familiar, clear, and joyous, rather like Walter Morel's morning extended temporally, spatially, and socially in all directions with perfect inclusiveness and every momentary adjustment of scale, from feelings as vividly private as Morel's through the exchanges of passionate love to the public grandeurs of the Trojan War. But all feelings are private and personal, the war is for Helen, Pandarus

---

[6]"His dapple-gray horse was in such a sweat it was something to look at; he seemed to have been running it for three miles. His yeoman's horse too was in such a sweat it could scarcely move. About its breastband the foam stood high; it was all flecked with foam, looking like a magpie. . . . He had been spurring his horse like a madman. He had a burdock-leaf under his hood to take the sweat and protect his head from the sun. But it was sheer joy to see him sweat! His forehead dripped like a still. . . ."

wouldn't do his thankless job if he didn't love both Troilus and Criseyde, love is the universal agent. Chaucer's irony—which doesn't undermine and set at odds, but binds and reconciles—is the sign of life that invites us into this world of light.

It's an irony free of guile, it doesn't give with one hand what it takes back with the other. When at the very beginning Criseyde, abandoned in Troy by her turncoat father and "wel neigh out of hir wit for sorwe and fere," comes to Hector pleading for mercy,

> Now was this Ector pitous of nature,
> And saugh that she was sorwfully bigon,
> And that she was so fair a creature;
> Of his goodnesse he gladede hire anon,
> And seyde, "Lat your fadres tresoun gon
> Forth with meschaunce, and ye youreself in joie
> Dwelleth with us, whil yow good list, in Troie. . . ."[7]

There are three distinct reasons, in descending order of importance, for Hector's response: (1) he is naturally merciful; (2) he sees that she is badly frightened; and (3) he sees that she is beautiful. The first reason is enough to ensure the substance of his response; the second ensures its gentleness; the third suffuses it with the superfluous and delightful warmth that any good man feels doing a disinterested good deed for a beautiful woman. Think of Fielding's "irony"—the leers and monkey tricks—breaking out in a comparable situation.

When Pandarus complicates his life by taking on the rôle of Troilus's envoy, advocate, mouthpiece, surrogate with Criseyde, he also complicates an old game, a domestic affection, a subliminal love affair of his own. Pandarus and Criseyde love each other as the amusing man-of-the-world uncle and the beautiful, unattached (she's a widow) courtly-lady niece; they enjoy the pleasure of each other's company; they gossip and joke and are comfortably familiar; they share the intimacy which confidently approaches and stops just this side of unex-

---

[7]"Now Hector was merciful by nature, and saw that she was in great distress, and that she was so fair a creature; out of his goodness he comforted her at once, and said, 'Let your father's treason go to the devil, and you yourself in joy dwell with us, as long as you please, in Troy. . . .' "

plorable possibilities. Pandarus will win for Troilus only if he avoids losing his own game. His advantages are his quick-wittedness, his ability to keep talking through the frostiest embarrassments, his assured sense—since he loves both Troilus and Criseyde—of the propriety of his mediation between them. His disadvantage is that, as all three of them know, in this sort of mediation even love isn't a good enough motive; that an uncle, however motivated, oughtn't to be promoting an affair which involves his niece. And Criseyde is a stubborn opponent, she is all alert resistance: Pandarus must prove every point and in effect prove it over again, as if it had never been proved, when he comes to the next one; in the game as Criseyde enforces the rules, Pandarus's sole alternative to another Sisyphean labor is a stroke of genius. So when Pandarus, having apparently cleared the way earlier, brings Criseyde her first letter from Troilus, she instantly reacts with fear and anger, reproachfully, in unfeigned opposition:

> Ful dredfully tho gan she stonden stylle,
> And took it naught, but al hire humble chere
> Gan for to chaunge, and seyde, "Scrit ne bille,
> For love of God, that toucheth swich matere,
> Ne brynge me noon; and also, uncle deere,
> To myn estat have more reward, I preye,
> Than to his lust! . . ."[8]

Whereupon Pandarus, having fulminated for a stanza or two against the incomprehensible finickiness of women, delivers his stroke of genius:

> "But thus ye faren, wel neigh alle and some,
> That he that most desireth yow to serve,
> Of hym ye recche leest wher he bycome,
> And whethir that he lyve or elles sterve.
> But for al that that ever I may deserve,
> Refuse it naught," quod he, and hente hire faste,
> And in hire bosom the lettre down he thraste,

---

[8]"Full of apprehension she stood motionless, and did not take it, but her easy manner changed, and she said, 'Bring me no letter or petition about such a matter, for the love of God; and also, dear uncle, have more regard for my honor, I beg you, than for his desire! . . .' "

And seyde hire, "Now cast it awey anon,
That folk may seen and gauren on us tweye."
Quod she, "I kan abyde til they be gon";
And gan to smyle, and seyde hym, "Em, I preye,
Swich answere as yow list youreself purveye,
For trewely I nyl no lettre write."
"No? than wol I," quod he, "so ye endite."

Therewith she lough, and seyde, "Go we dyne."
And he gan at hymself to jape faste,
And seyde, "Nece, I have so gret a pyne
For love, that everich other day I faste—"
And gan his beste japes forth to caste,
And made hire so to laughe at his folye,
That she for laughter wende for to dye.[9]

Pandarus has made Point One over again, he has made Point Two via special-delivery, and he and Criseyde stroll off together laughing toward the not yet formulated Point Three, with the somewhat agitated hearts of lovers and friends who know that the unfinishable game is worthy of them both.

Chaucer's irony doesn't demand scapegoats, it isn't a judgment of the stupidity or self-deception or wickedness of

---

[9] " 'But so you carry on, nearly the whole lot of you, that the one who most desires to serve you, what becomes of him matters least to you, and whether he lives or dies. But for all I may ever have coming to me, don't refuse it,' he said, and held her fast, and thrust the letter down into her bosom, and said to her, 'Now throw it away at once, so that people can see and gape at both of us.' Said she, 'I can wait till they're gone'; and smiled, and said to him, 'Uncle, I beg you, such answer as you would like provide by yourself, for truly I will write no letter.' 'No? then I will,' said he, 'so long as you dictate.' At that she laughed, and said, 'Let's go to dinner.' And he kept making jokes at his own expense, and said, 'Niece, I have such great torment for love that every other day I fast—' and brought out his best jokes, and made her laugh so hard at his foolishness that she thought she would die laughing." Scholars who have heard that Chaucer's source for *Troilus and Criseyde* is Boccaccio's *Il Filostrato*, but haven't read it, will be relieved to learn that here—and in the other passages cited in this essay—Chaucer is either inventing out of thin air or, as in this case, converting a platitude into a stroke of genius. Boccaccio's platitude: "Somewhat troubled by this, Pandarus said: '. . . I have spoken to thee so much of this, thou shouldst not now be over-nice with me. I pray thee, do not deny me this now.' Criseida smiled as she heard him, and took the letter and put it in her bosom. Then she said to him: 'When I find time I shall read it as best I can. . . .' "

others. It's a road map, rather, of the twists and turns and abrupt halts by which everybody hopes to come out sooner or later straight (as when Criseyde freezes till Pandarus finds the right way of posting the letter); or it may be a bit of *double-entendre* to emphasize that life is complex even when in the heat of emotion somebody considers it simple (Troilus, lamenting Criseyde's absence, apostrophizes her palace: "O thow lanterne of which queynt is the light"—"queynt" meaning "quenched," but also heard by the reader, though at the moment certainly not by Troilus, as the vulgar word for the female genitals); or it may be a reminder of personal claims that, attentive only to love, lovers can at some peril to their humanity neglect and ignore. Chaucer's best instance of such a reminder is so quiet and brief, and so subordinated in the text to the excitement of what is about to happen, that arriving at it readers usually don't, though they should, stop short.

The instance occurs at the center of the poem, toward the center of Book III, just before the lovers are brought to bed together. Criseyde, still refractory to anything more drastic than fine speeches, has been invited by Pandarus to spend the evening in his house, at a time for which the astrological signs, as Pandarus interprets them, promise heavy rain. The storm will justify his persuading Criseyde to stay, and its racket will cover other sounds and talk in the night. Criseyde comes (she doesn't know, but may well surmise, that Troilus is already on the premises, concealed and trembling somewhere), it pours and thunders, and Criseyde agrees to spend the night. Pandarus does everything but draw diagrams as he explains the arrangements that will put Criseyde off in a room by herself; in the next room, the only one directly accessible to hers, beyond an open door will be her attendant ladies; in the room on the other side of theirs, Pandarus (this is a medieval house, without corridors). It appears, then, that Criseyde is effectively isolated for the night; and, though Chaucer doesn't record Criseyde's reactions, he may intend us to assume that at the start of the evening she is full of expectation and prepared to continue holding out, later puzzled and perhaps disappointed, finally resigned to the prospect of an untroubled sleep.

In the middle of the night Pandarus goes to fetch Troilus, drags this "wrecched mouses herte" through a trap-door into Criseyde's room, softly closes the door on the sleeping women in the next room,

> And as he com ayeynward pryvely,
> His nece awook, and axed, "Who goth there?"
> "My dere nece," quod he, "it am I.
> Ne wondreth nought, ne have of it no fere."
> And ner he com, and seyde hire in hire ere,
> "No word, for love of God, I yow biseche!
> Lat no wight risen and heren of oure speche."
>
> "What! which wey be ye comen, *benedicite*?"
> Quod she, "and how thus unwist of hem alle?"
> "Here at this secre trappe-dore," quod he.
> Quod tho Criseyde, "Lat me som wight calle!"
> "I! God forbede that it sholde falle,"
> Quod Pandarus, "that ye swich folye wroughte!
> They myghte demen thyng they nevere er thoughte.
>
> "It is nought good a slepyng hound to wake,
> Ne yeve a wight a cause to devyne.
> Youre wommen slepen alle, I undertake,
> So that, for hem, the hous men myghte myne,
> And slepen wollen til the sonne shyne.
> And whan my tale brought is to an ende,
> Unwist, right as I com, so wol I wende. . . ."

And Pandarus goes on to improvise his story about Troilus (who all this time has been cowering, undiscovered by Criseyde, in a corner of the room), a lie that proves to be the last link in Pandarus's great chain of persuasion. Meanwhile the three preliminary stanzas quoted above are liable to slip past unexamined as the reader and the lovers sweep toward the long deferred event.

Nothing slips past Chaucer, however; least of all, anybody's claim and right to be noticed. Loved and admired and (more or less) heeded as he is from the beginning by both Troilus and Criseyde, Pandarus at once becomes the necessary instrument—compliant and sensitive no doubt, but instrument nevertheless—of their conjunction. All this time he has subordinated himself utterly to what they are bound to do, and now that they are about to do it he is programmed to shut himself off like a good little machine. One move is left for him, his transcendently lonely and most dangerous risk. Troilus for the present is an emotional basket-case ready for nothing but love, and Criseyde is radiantly ready to give him anything but love. Pandarus concludes that only a really spectacular invention— say, a faked crisis, an astounding lie in the middle of the night, with Troilus available for immediate transfer into her bed— will have a chance of overwhelming and defeating her. But what can Pandarus say at that moment when Criseyde awakens, in the dark, to find her uncle apparently alone with her in the room he has so elaborately arranged for her to be undisturbed in? "Who's there?" she says. "My dear niece," he replies, identifying himself and using the reassuring word of affection, "it's me. Don't wonder or be afraid." And he comes nearer and whispers in her ear, "Not a word, for the love of God, I beseech you! Don't let anyone get up and hear what we're saying." Criseyde, by now completely alert and uneasy but not yet certain whether she should be alarmed, asks, "How did you get in without their knowing?" "Here, at this secret trap-door." "Let me call somebody," says Criseyde.

She has virtually decided to be alarmed. If she calls to her women, of course not only Pandarus's plan but Pandarus himself will be ruined. She must now, it seems, decide that her uncle, who has always been loving and useful, is turning out to be more loving than she had thought; that, pretending to be speaking for Troilus (John Alden for the tongue-tied soldier Captain Standish), he has in fact been speaking for himself (he too is human, as it's a shock to recall, he too has desires, he isn't a machine, people expect to be paid for their labor and their love, maybe he hasn't tacitly accepted the limit beyond which nothing); and, if her suspicions are well grounded, then even an awful scandal—what will the women think as they rush into the room where in the dead of night Pandarus stands by Criseyde's bed?—is preferable to the alternative. "God forbid," says Pandarus, "that you should commit such a folly! They might think what they never thought before." Providentially, Criseyde isn't a flighty or hysterical woman, and Pandarus keeps talking calmly and sensibly: "It isn't good to wake a sleeping dog [Pandarus's lust? the women's malice?], nor to give anybody cause to speculate. Your women are all asleep, I give you my word, so that, as far as they're concerned, the house might be about to fall down and they'll sleep till the sun shines. And when my tale is brought to an end, without anyone's knowing, just as I came, so will I leave." The danger is past, the cock-and-bull story about Troilus's "jealousy" redirects Criseyde's attention back to her will-I-won't-I dilemma, Pandarus can be forgotten again by readers and lovers except as the necessary instrument, and the momentarily immobilized —as if during the blink of an eye—narrative resumes its not quite imperturbable journey.

For a moment, though, Chaucer raises Pandarus's personal claim (as Kafka raised Kellermann's). Pandarus is possibility, the path not followed, what might have happened if the world were as crazy as it is (the audience would leap up as one woman with torrential applause and shout, "It's only you we love, Bernhard Kellermann! So give us another six or eight of those unpublished things from your pen!"), what mostly it's better not to muse over because people ought to know their place and stay there (out of the picture). Kellermann and Pandarus are both sublime because each inconveniently exists, in defiance of other people's tastes and impulses. The difference between them is that Kellermann doesn't know his place and Pandarus does: Kellermann is the comic sublime; Pandarus in the course of the poem is many things besides, but at this moment he is the tragic sublime. The way to dispose of such figures is to say that they are "larger than life"—which is an inadvertent way of saying that, in the world as well as in fiction, Kellermann is larger than all the life-size and circumambient machinery.

II.
Lawrence

Lawrence's relation to the great Russians, whom he like everybody else read and marveled at when young, is camouflaged by the ferocity with which he repudiated them. Dostoevsky became Lawrence's particular target, the enemy of light, "the rat, slithering along in hate, in the shadows, and, in order to belong to the light, professing love, all love. . . . He is not nice." Tolstoy was "old Leo," the self-tormenting moralist, the man who lost his nerve, who condemned his deepest feelings, betrayed his passionate nature ("wetted on the flame of his own manhood") by insisting that social forms were the measure of life—by pretending, for instance, that the house-pet Pierre was something and the soldier Vronsky nothing. Moreover the Russians, lumped together, would have to take the blame for inventing the soul:

> That's why the Russians are so popular. No matter how much of a shabby animal you may be, you can learn from Dostoievsky and Tchekhov, etc., how to have the most tender, unique, coruscating soul on earth. And so you may be most vastly important to yourself. Which is the private aim of all men. The hero had it openly. The commonplace person has it inside himself, though outwardly he says: Of course I'm no better than anybody else! His very asserting it shows he doesn't

think it for a second. Every character in Dostoievsky or Tchek-
hov thinks himself *inwardly* a nonesuch, absolutely unique.

(Did Lawrence know that in Russian "soul" was also a euphemism for "male serf": e.g., in Gogol's *Dead Souls*?) Against
such formidable and seductive enemies, one had to be unrelent-
ing. "Oh, don't think I would belittle the Russians," he wrote
to a friend in 1916 (he was thirty-one, and had nearly completed the final draft of his most Russian novel, *Women in Love*).
"They have meant an enormous amount to me; Turgenev, Tolstoi, Dostoievsky—mattered almost more than anything, and I
thought them the greatest writers of all time. And now, with
something of a shock, I realise a certain crudity and thick, uncivilised, insensitive stupidity about them, I realise how much
finer and purer and more ultimate our own stuff is." The emphatic word is "ultimate" because it's the word likely to be
flaunted by admirers of the Russians, especially of Dostoevsky;
and Lawrence emphasizes it again in his largest, bristliest, and
most brilliant statement of repudiation (written in 1920, as the
beginning of his Preface to Shestov's *All Things Are Possible*):

In his paragraph on The Russian Spirit, Shestov gives us
the real clue to Russian literature. European culture is a root-
less thing in the Russians. With us, it is our very blood and
bones, the very nerve and root of our psyche. We think in a certain fashion, we feel in a certain fashion, because our whole substance is of this fashion. Our speech and feeling are organically
inevitable to us.

With the Russians it is different. They have only been inoc-
ulated with the virus of European culture and ethic. The virus
works in them like a disease. And the inflammation and irrita-
tion comes forth as literature. The bubbling and fizzing is almost chemical, not organic. It is an organism seething as it ac-
cepts and masters the strange virus. What the Russian is
struggling with, crying out against, is not life itself: it is only
European culture which has been introduced into his psyche,
and which hurts him. The tragedy is not so much a real soul
tragedy, as a surgical one. Russian art, Russian literature after
all does not stand on the same footing as European and Greek
or Egyptian art. It is not spontaneous utterance. It is not the
flowering of a race. It is a surgical outcry, horrifying, or mar-

vellous, lacerating at first; but when we get used to it, not really
so profound, not really ultimate, a little extraneous.

So the Russians are "a little extraneous" to "European
culture," and Lawrence has a clear field. The only other writer
as unlimited and authoritative in his judgments of big names
and entire cultures is Tolstoy (Lawrence's "old Leo," the repudiated father), who denounces the French, the Germans, modern art, Symbolism, Impressionism, Naturalism, the Deca-
dents, Ibsen, Wagner, Nietzsche, Baudelaire, Verlaine,
Mallarmé, Shakespeare as exuberantly as Lawrence denounces
many on the same list plus many others—the Americans, the
Italians, the Australians, the English, men, women, the young,
the old—and of course the Russians (from whom nobody
learned more than their denouncer). Harry T. Moore, however,
doesn't find the parallel interesting enough to bring up in his
biography of Lawrence.[1] Moore mentions Tolstoy only five
times, always in passing, though one would expect a biographer
to be alerted by the fact he offers, in passing, that Lawrence in
his early twenties—by the end of his twenties he had written almost all his major fiction—still "believed that *Anna Karenina*
was the greatest of novels." Logan Speirs has an excellent
chapter[2] on the indebtedness of *The Rainbow* to *Anna
Karenina*: these "two massive studies of marriage," with such
closely related characters as Levin/Tom Brangwen and
Vronsky/Skrebensky; not that Lawrence is ever imitating or
duplicating—the connection isn't originals-and-copies but
fathers-and-sons, new locales for the same immortal germ
plasm. *Women in Love* (which Speirs doesn't discuss) is another "massive study of marriage," and its two contrasting
pairs of lovers—the doomed and the fortunate—are evidently
descended from Anna-Vronsky and Kitty-Levin. The doubly
Russian peculiarity of *Women in Love*, though, is that while its
ostensible subject is Tolstoyan, its tone and structure are Dostoevskian: after the unhurried and multitudinous narrative of
The Rainbow, bursts of apocalyptic talk alternating with bursts

---

[1] *The Priest of Love* (New York, 1974).

[2] In his excellent study, *Tolstoy and Chekhov* (Cambridge, 1971).

of disruptive action; abrupt and unrationalized changes of
mood; reciprocally destructive relationships such as the one between Gudrun and Gerald, who are fighting the hopeless war
that Nastasya fought with Myshkin and Rogozhin in *The
Idiot*. The question of *The Rainbow* (as of *Anna Karenina*) is,
What is the meaning of life and marriage? whereas the question
of *Women in Love* (as of any Dostoevsky novel) is, What is the
meaning of death and dissolution? In *The Rainbow* and
Women in Love, Lawrence is the first English novelist to pose
the cosmic questions, and he had nobody to learn from except
the Russians. Or, as Speirs states the case specifically for
Lawrence and Tolstoy:

> Both Tolstoy and Lawrence seek in their art to arrive at some
> definition of fulfilment in life. They both see life as a quest for
> spiritual illumination which must be made anew by each indi-
> vidual in his own way according to his generation and his cir-
> cumstances. They both believe that any illumination which is at-
> tained can only be made perfect when a man and a woman have
> come together in their lives. These conceptions underlie their
> great art. Starting from them, they travelled along widely diver-
> gent paths. But Lawrence always understood Tolstoy very well.
> One can see this beneath his harshest criticisms. He said of him:
> "Count Tolstoi had that last weakness of a great man: he want-
> ed the absolute."

So did Lawrence, and there isn't room for more than one
absolutist at a time.

For Tolstoy and Lawrence, literature had to be tested by
life and, for both of them, it eventually failed the test. Tolstoy
staked everything on marriage—his own, that is—and lost.
Anna Karenina was the last novel he could possibly have written while still clinging by his fingernails to the notion that marriage is possible (and it's the greatest novel about marriage).
Within months after completing it—he wasn't yet fifty—he had
almost given up on life and had been very near suicide, as he
disclosed in "A Confession"; soon and for the rest of his long
life, he had given up on marriage, women, sex, meat, alcohol,
violence, and such vicious trivialities as *Anna Karenina* (when
admirers came to old Leo with praise of *Anna Karenina*, he re-

torted: "What difficulty is there in writing about how an officer fell in love with a married woman? there's no difficulty in it, and, above all, no good in it"; when they begged him for "another *War and Peace*," he exclaimed that "it's like asking an old whore to fling up her skirts and dance!"). Of course he remained the best writer in the world, and every once in a while, whenever he got restless or exasperated enough to take a break from turning out his tracts for the times (which are as fresh and straightforward as one would expect from the best writer in the world), he would produce a monomaniacal masterpiece like *The Death of Ivan Ilych* or an antidote to *Anna Karenina* like *The Kreutzer Sonata* or a miraculously clear-eyed adventure story like *Hadji Murad* (written in his seventies) or a jeremiad against Shakespeare, Wagner, and their innumerable company of bogus artists.

Lawrence, on the other hand, staked everything on marriage and won. In the five years following his elopement with Frieda, he wrote *Sons and Lovers, The Rainbow*, and *Women in Love*, which can be called without sheer absurdity the three best English novels of the twentieth century. Yet *Women in Love* was for Lawrence very much like what *Anna Karenina* had been for Tolstoy: it was the last possible novel Lawrence could have written while he still believed in the notion of marriage that had sustained him through those prodigious years. At thirty-one, he would live another thirteen years and write thousands of letters as vivid as any in the world and dozens of volumes of fiction, poetry, travel, psychology, prophecy, arcane speculation, archeology, anthropology, and the most incandescent literary criticism in English, but he would never write another good novel or even any short stories up to the level of the dozen or more wonderful stories he had written during his twenties. In "Why the Novel Matters" Lawrence proudly called himself a novelist and the novel "the one bright book of life"—

. . . I am a novelist. And being a novelist, I consider myself superior to the saint, the scientist, the philosopher, and the poet, who are all great masters of different bits of man alive, but never get the whole hog.

The novel is the one bright book of life. Books are not life. They are only tremulations on the ether. But the novel as a tremulation can make the whole man alive tremble. Which is more than poetry, philosophy, science, or any other book-tremulation can do.

—but he could hardly have said (or believed) that he had stopped being a novelist years before, that "the one bright book of life" would have to be written by others now, that Lawrence himself was only the brightest of the reflective on-lookers. At forty, writing *Lady Chatterley's Lover*, the feeble and spiteful novel with which he intended to glorify "the phallic consciousness," he was already (if Frieda's complaint to her friends, as Moore reports it, can be trusted) impotent.[3] The phallic consciousness had become an idea in a book ("Books are not life"). No doubt what Lawrence always referred to as his "bronchial" ailment—it was never anything else till he died of tuberculosis—had something to do with the sudden decline. No doubt the suppression of *The Rainbow*, the consequent delay in the publication of *Women in Love*, and Lawrence's failure to come into his rightful inheritance and be accepted as the greatest living English novelist had something to do with it. The First World War—which Lawrence considered the death of hope for Europe—no doubt angered, infuriated, troubled, depressed, perhaps even *diminished* him; he often said so; though public disasters are handy as surrogates for the private

---

[3]One of those Russians had already stated the case with "a certain crudity"—Chekhov, aged thirty-three, untactfully explaining to his friend Suvorin, aged fifty-nine, why Zola shouldn't have written about a young woman who falls in love with an old man: "It hurts me to read about Clotilde being screwed by Pascal instead of someone younger and stronger. . . . And what nonsense! Is potency a sign of true life and health? Is screwing the only thing that makes one a real person? All thinkers are impotent at forty, while ninety-year-old savages keep ninety wives apiece. . . ." But then Chekhov (for whom Lawrence's final formula of repudiation was: "a second-rate writer and a willy wet-leg") had anticipated Lawrence in other ways: by flaming into literary prominence in his twenties; by charming almost everybody and being content with almost nobody; by traveling much of his life all over Europe (and across Asia; though not, like Lawrence, to Australia and America also) in search of a cure for traveling; by changing the nature of the short story for his time and for all time; by burning out at forty-four with tuberculosis.

agonies that the agonist is trying to forget but at least would rather not talk about or allow in the line of sight.

Moore tucks into a sub-section of his book with the inscrutable title "Strife and Scholarship" a half-dozen skittish pages on Lawrence's sexuality (summed up by the biographer with a numerical conclusion from Richard Aldington, who "stated in a letter of March 16, 1960, 'I should say D.H.L. was about 85 per cent hetero and 15 per cent homo' "):

> Compton Mackenzie claims, in his autobiography, . . . that Lawrence told him, "I believe that the nearest I've ever come to perfect love was with a young coal-miner when I was about sixteen." If this is precisely what he said, he could hardly have been referring to Alan Chambers, a farm boy, though Chambers may have gone into the pits later. . . .
>
> [The] . . . friendship passages between the Lawrence hero and another male, not only in earlier but also in some of the later novels, have caused a raising of eyebrows but, despite all innuendoes, Lawrence doesn't seem to have been a homosexual; at least not a complete or continually practicing one. Frieda Lawrence used to insist that her husband was not in any way a homosexual, but towards the end of her life she changed her tune somewhat; as she wrote in 1949 to Edward Gilbert, who was studying Lawrence, "Murry and he had no 'love affair.' But he did not disbelieve in homosexuality." Not long afterwards, Frieda wrote to Murry that she was sure Lawrence had had no homosexual feeling for him, that Lawrence's homosexuality had lasted only a brief time (apparently in the World War I days of the Cornish farmer), and that she had fought with him over it, and had won.
>
> Certainly no one spoke out on sexual matters more boldly and clearly than Lawrence, and there is no passage in his works in which he writes approvingly of *sexual* relations, that is, of sexual gratification, between men. Indeed, he writes disapprovingly of such things, though in the unused "Prologue" to *Women in Love* . . . Birkin's inclinations seem definitely homosexual. Yet how much of this reflects Lawrence himself is problematic. (In the film made from the novel, the director erred in giving Birkin a beard, like the author's, which Lawrence hadn't done. Birkin may have been somewhat of a spokesman for the author, but he was not the author himself.) . . .

This is how Moore's typewriter goes rattling along, its eyebrows raised and lowered by innuendo and disclaimer, homo and hetero, Birkin's razor and Lawrence's beard, sex and love (the phoenix and the turtle), getting your kicks minus chicks in the Cornish sticks (the phoenix turned turtle), strife and scholarship at the tricky flicks. It's a dizzying ride, and Moore never comes off it long enough to notice, in *Women in Love* and elsewhere, an instructive peculiarity of Lawrence's descriptions of people—that a woman is the clothes she wears (sometimes specified with a dressmaker's eye, as in the description of Gudrun on page 2 of *Women in Love*) and a man is his body (as if he wears no clothes at all):

> "Ah-h-h!" came her strange, intaken cry, as, on the reflex, she started, turned and fled, scudding with an unthinkable swift beating of her white feet and fraying of her white garments, towards the church. Like a hound the young man was after her, leaping the steps and swinging past her father, his supple haunches working like those of a hound that bears down on the quarry.

Here, in the wedding scene of the opening chapter of *Women in Love* (the bride's "white feet" are her shoes, and the bridegroom, one hopes, is fully clothed), it's nobody but the omniscient author giving his view of things; and readers will remember that Birkin's thighs, flanks, and loins play an important role in the author's presentation of the love scene with Ursula later on. As for Birkin's relation to the author, Birkin may lack Lawrence's beard but, in the novel Lawrence published, Birkin expresses just about every attitude and opinion Lawrence was expressing elsewhere at the time in his own person; and the "unused 'Prologue' " to *Women in Love* seems to have been intended as a sober and explicit account of the deepest feelings of the character who will be much more than "somewhat of a spokesman" for his author:

> All the time, he recognized that, although he was always drawn to women, feeling more at home with a woman than with a man, yet it was for men that he felt the hot, flushing, roused attraction which a man is supposed to feel for the other sex. Although nearly all his living interchange went on with one

woman or another, although he was always terribly intimate with at least one woman, and practically never intimate with a man, yet the male physique had a fascination for him, and for the female physique he felt only a fondness, a sort of sacred love, as for a sister. . . .

He wanted all the time to love women. He wanted all the while to feel this kindled, loving attraction towards a beautiful woman, that he would often feel towards a handsome man. But he could not. Whenever it was a case of a woman, there entered in too much spiritual, sisterly love; or else, in reaction, there was only a brutal, callous sort of lust.

This was an entanglement from which there seemed no escape. How can a man *create* his own feelings? He cannot. It is only in his power to suppress them, to bind them in the chain of the will. And what is suppression but a mere negation of life, and of living.

He had several friendships wherein this passion entered, friendships with men of no very great intelligence, but of pleasant appearance: ruddy, well-nourished fellows, good-natured and easy, who protected him in his delicate health more gently than a woman would protect him. He loved his friend, the beauty of whose manly limbs made him tremble with pleasure. He wanted to caress him.

But reserve, which was as strong as a chain of iron in him, kept him from any demonstration. And if he were away for any length of time from the man he loved so hotly, then he forgot him, the flame which invested the beloved like a transfiguration passed away, and Birkin remembered his friend as tedious. He could not go back to him, to talk as tediously as he would have to talk, to take such a level of intelligence as he would have to take. He forgot his men friends completely, as one forgets the candle one has blown out. . . .

Birkin is telling all, and it's much more than we need to know for fiction:

It might be any man, a policeman who suddenly looked up at him, as he inquired the way, or a soldier who sat next to him in a railway carriage. How vividly, months afterwards, he would recall the soldier who had sat pressed up close to him on a journey from Charing Cross to Westerham; the shapely, motionless body, the large, dumb, coarsely-beautiful hands that rested helpless upon the strong knees, the dark brown eyes, vulnerable in the erect body. . . .

The preoccupations are Birkin's (or Lawrence's), but the voice could be out of an earlier "Confession," the voice of old Leo, condemning his deepest feelings yet superbly unregenerate at the heart of his *mea culpa*, attentive and full of thought, father, guide, fellow-victim, self-tormenting judge, spirit trapped in the wayward flesh:

> He wanted to cast out these desires, he wanted not to know them. Yet a man can no more slay a living desire in him, than he can prevent his body from feeling heat and cold. He can put himself into bondage, to prevent the fulfilment of the desire, that is all. But the desire is there, as the travelling of the blood itself is there, until it is fulfilled or until the body is dead.
>
> So he went on, month after month, year after year, divided against himself, striving for the day when the beauty of men should not be so acutely attractive to him, when the beauty of woman should move him instead. . . .
>
> But then, inevitably, it would recur again. There would come into a restaurant a strange Cornish type of man, with dark eyes like holes in his head, or like the eyes of a rat, and with dark, fine, rather stiff hair, and full, heavy, softly-strong limbs. Then again Birkin would feel the desire spring up in him, the desire to know this man, to have him, as it were to eat him, to take the very substance of him. And watching the strange, rather furtive, rabbit-like way in which the strong, softly-built man ate, Birkin would feel the rousedness burning in his own breast, as if this were what he wanted, as if the satisfaction of his desire lay in the body of the young, strong man opposite.
>
> And then in his soul would succeed a sort of despair, because this passion for a man had recurred in him. It was a deep misery to him. And it would seem as if he had always loved men, always and only loved men. And this was the greatest suffering to him. . . .
>
> This was the one and only secret he kept to himself, this secret of his passionate and sudden, spasmodic affinity for men he saw. He kept this secret even from himself. He knew what he felt, but he always kept the knowledge at bay. His a priori were: "I *should not* feel like this," and "It is the ultimate mark of my own deficiency, that I feel like this." Therefore, though he ad-

mitted everything, he never really faced the question. He never accepted the desire, and received it as part of himself. He always tried to keep it expelled from him.

Lawrence decided to keep Birkin's secret after all (as for Tolstoy's secret, maybe it could be made public almost at once because it came complete with a happy ending in Christian asceticism), and he excised the Prologue from its place at the beginning of *Women in Love*. The Prologue remained in manuscript till it was published separately in 1963.

Women in Love is, then, at least in fact a decapitated novel. It has splendid sustained episodes (especially the chapter "Water-Party," the best stretch of densely populated and thematically coherent narrative Lawrence ever wrote); it has the most intense love-affair in Lawrence's fiction, not a polarity or a blood-sympathy but the Dostoevskian torrent of ill-fated passion between Gudrun and Gerald (with Loerke—"like a rat in the river of corruption," says Birkin; like "the strange Cornish type of man . . . with the eyes of a rat" that the *ur*-Birkin of the Prologue yearned for; like Lawrence's fascinated impression of the prince of darkness Dostoevsky himself—the lurker waiting in the dark, all ears and eyes, for the heavens to fall); it has the great concluding scenes of death on the ice-mountains and unresolvable doubt in the survivor; and it has many mysteries or ambiguities of tone and structure that look, and up to a point really are, Dostoevskian—Europe at the end of its tether—but that seem to be also elisions and omissions of what Lawrence couldn't quite bring himself to say about more intimate questions. It is never, for instance, altogether clear what Birkin wants; nor is it altogether clear that Birkin doesn't entirely know what he wants; and the chapter "Gladiatorial," in which Birkin and Gerald wrestle naked, engages not only the two friends but the casuistical ingenuity of scores of Lawrence critics without nullifying everybody's suspicion that the explanation is simple, and would be simpler still if Lawrence had kept the bleak and brave Prologue and allowed his novel to flow unhappily out of it. At any rate, after *Women in Love*, Lawrence was finished as a novelist. The three "leadership" novels that follow would be politically offensive if they weren't as feeble as *Lady Chatterley's Lover*; and all four of them are as malicious and theoretical as Sir Joshua, Lawrence's carica-ture of Bertrand Russell in *Women in Love*.

Moore, however, doing a bit of criticism in his critical bi-ography, rates *Lady Chatterley's Lover* very high. True, he has a reservation about the plot, which doesn't give Sir Clifford enough time for reading ("It would have been a stronger story if Lawrence had made Clifford's lack of sex the result of overintellectualization"), and he has a reservation about what he calls the "prose," which would be bad if it were thin and good if it were plump but confusingly is neither ("not yet the thinned, satiric writing most characteristic of that last period, but on the other hand it is not the full-bodied prose of the novels from *Sons and Lovers* to *The Plumed Serpent*"); none-theless, "purely on its own merits" it is "one of the notable books of the century." Moore is a sort of dualist: something he variously designates as "prose" or "style" or "language" or "magic of expression" often finds its way, he believes, into Lawrence's books. *The Plumed Serpent*, for example, "con-tains some of Lawrence's finest prose," though not the "stylis-tic mastery" of *The Rainbow*. *Studies in American Literature* contains a "colloquial idiom" which—as thick and convex as the Coke-bottle lenses of a mad scientist's pince-nez—"lets through more intensity than the flat prose of scholarship usual-ly transmits" (n.b. the scholarly caution of that adverb); whereas when Mabel Luhan proclaims her "semi-Lawrencean ideas" they "sound . . . rather hollow without Lawrence's magic of expression." Which became ever more magical: one of the remarkable facts about Lawrence as he grew up from early childhood and kept on with his "prose" was (Moore notes) "his increasing skill in the use of language," though he never again "achieved the integration of art and idea that he manifested in *The Rainbow* and *Women in Love*." Inside this two-ply but integrated sarcophagus lies poor dead Lawrence grinding his teeth to powder.

Moore the literary critic on (what else?) Lawrence's limi-tations as a literary critic: "he couldn't 'forgive Conrad for being so sad and for giving in.' He also said that he hated

Strindberg, who seemed 'unnatural, forced, a bit indecent—a
bit wooden, like Ibsen, a bit skin-erupty,' remarks indicating
that in literary judgments Lawrence was at times somewhat
limited." Vincent van Moore on Lawrence's limitations as an
art critic: "Lawrence—quite wrongly, as time has shown—
carped at these paintings [murals by Rivera and Orozco]."
Harry T. Carp on Lawrence's limitations as a philosopher:
"One of the new ideas or symbols Lawrence was trying to
grasp through his writing was that of darkness; it was to become an important one to him, along with that of 'the blood.'
Lawrence was never a formal philosopher; nevertheless . . ."
(if the prince turned into a frog and nobody told him, he would
have something like Moore's majestic presumptuousness).

Since Lawrence wasn't a "formal" psychologist either
(most writers can't tell their id from their elbow), it's surprising
that Moore finds so many ideas of Lawrence's to be kind
about: e.g., Lawrence in his aspect of doctrinaire windbag and
sexy symbolist: " 'Sun' . . . embodies much of his essential
doctrine, dramatized through [such] symbolism" as "the sleeping (sexually unawakened) woman." Yet, amateur though he
was, he may well have been one of the first two writers who
discovered that letters could be written in prose: "That letter
. . ., which was written at a period when Lawrence was not reg-
ularly exercising his imaginative faculty [it was during his
visit to Finland, where he got his head caught in the door of a
sauna], had the force of a creative essay. Lawrence perhaps
realized, as Rilke [a famous Austrian writer] did, that letters
could be creative." Moreover, though never a *formal* writer,
Lawrence was quite a modern one: " 'The Rocking-Horse Win-
ner' . . . indicates Lawrence's modernness of method, for . . . he
was among the first writers of his time who drew upon anthropology." Nor was he content to stop at modernness, but forged
ahead to become modernistic as well: "In the latter half [of
The Rainbow] there is a new Lawrence . . . the Lawrence who
became modernistic along with Joyce and Proust"—as in
Ursula's "grainfield episode with Skrebensky, which seems
part early Stravinsky and part later Van Gogh, yet most originally Lawrencean." And so amid this shower of droppings

he turned at last into a Name: "Here [in Lawrence's Diamond-and-carbon letter to Edward Garnett[4]],"

> in an important moment, a moment of culmination, Lawrence showed that he knew what he was doing, and why he was doing it. He had reached a plateau of understanding from which he could see his writing in relation to the world about him. It was a world whose thoughts had been shaped, were being shaped, by Darwin, Marx, Einstein, and Freud [The *Top* Names], whose influence no one could really evade. Artistically, it was a world that would soon belong to Stravinsky, Picasso, and Joyce. As Lawrence didn't take anything important from the Futurists, so he consciously took nothing from these artists—indeed, he cared little for their achievements—but once again, his work, like theirs, demonstrates a modernity of vision. . . .

Moore is encyclopedic in range but telegraphic in manner: he never takes the trouble to discuss or illustrate these influences and associations; roll-calls are enough, and the less sense the better. (It ought to be acknowledged that he is here and there if not by and large a robust writer, and as the names pour incontinently out he has occasional lapses of taste: for instance, describes Mrs. Luhan's husband as "the massive Indian-buck

---

[4]"When Marinetti writes: 'It is the solidity of a blade of steel that is interesting by itself, that is, the incomprehending and inhuman alliance of its molecules in resistance to, let us say, a bullet. The heat of a piece of wood or iron is in fact more passionate, for us, than the laughter or tears of a woman'— then I know what he means. He is stupid, as an artist, for contrasting the heat of the iron and the laugh of the woman. Because what is interesting in the laugh of the woman is the same as the binding of the molecules of steel or their action in heat: it is the inhuman will, call it physiology, or like Marinetti—physiology of matter, that fascinates me. . . . You mustn't look in my novel for the old stable *ego* of the character. There is another *ego*, according to whose action the individual is unrecognisable, and passes through, as it were, allotropic states which it needs a deeper sense than any we've been used to exercise, to discover are states of the same single radically unchanged element. (Like as diamond and coal are the same pure single element of carbon. The ordinary novel would trace the history of the diamond—but I say, 'Diamond, what! This is carbon.' And my diamond might be coal or soot, and my theme is carbon.)" In the same letter Lawrence doesn't forget to take his by now ritualistic swipe at the Russians: "In Turgenev, and in Tolstoi, and in Dostoievsky, the moral scheme into which all the characters fit—and it is nearly the same scheme—is, whatever the extraordinariness of the characters themselves, dull, old, dead."

lover she had acquired" and, again, "her Indian-buck lover"; or romantically allows as how "Jessie Chambers was an almost classical case of frigidity"; but nobody's perfect, and very few are even modernistic.) People who don't read Lawrence can learn all about him from Moore.

Anybody with an "essential doctrine" deserves such followers and will not fail to carry them along like fleas. Tolstoy had them, a tribulation named Chertkov in particular; so did Jesus. Lawrence (Lorenzo the Insignificant) celebrated his Last Supper with the disciples at the Café Royal on a visit he made to London in 1924: "at one point Murry said, 'I love you, Lorenzo, but I won't promise not to betray you'—and finally the 'habitually temperate' Lawrence collapsed, sick and vomiting." Every now and then, as at the Last Supper, Lawrence did some strenuous recruiting for a utopian-anarchist commune of love and brotherhood, to be named Rananim, which he hoped to establish in Florida or somewhere else remote (where he himself would have been ineluctably more equal than the others). Moore's deficiencies of perception, proportion, tone, taste, judgment in his insulting book don't help; but—once Lawrence had had the good sense to run off with the one woman in the world he couldn't beat down or turn into an echo or talk out of being a bossy, brassy woman—most of the friendships and many of the events of his life don't make for pleasant reading or contemplation either in Moore's book or wherever else they appear in print. When *The Intelligent Heart* was published twenty years ago (*The Priest of Love* is its most recent revision), Frieda wrote that it "reads almost like fiction, and a great deal is fiction to me":

> Lawrence and I lived often for weeks and months in peace in the midst of a terrific turmoil and gossip that we were not aware of. So much spite against two unpretentious people who lived as simply as we did. But somehow it did not matter much; we went on our way in our world. A man's new ideas are not so easy to grasp right away and it makes people hostile. There were a few like Aldous and Maria Huxley who patiently listened.

And Lawrence was always on the lookout for listeners.

He was also always on the lookout for things to tell them, even at his pushiest. In the early 'twenties Lawrence was at the very bottom of his funk: his two best novels had fallen dead for their time, and he was trying without luck to find a way of making fiction out of leader-and-follower politics. His essay *Psychoanalysis and the Unconscious*—a jargon-stuffed, deliberately nutty, sporadically lively effort to correct what he considered Freud's moralistic attitude toward the unconscious—had been treated as a bad joke by reviewers; and Lawrence plunged ahead into *Fantasia of the Unconscious*, which begins with the three hysterical pages of its so-called Foreword:

> The present book is a continuation from *Psychoanalysis and the Unconscious*. The generality of readers had better just leave it alone. The generality of critics likewise. I really don't want to convince anybody. It is quite in opposition to my whole nature. . . .
>
> I warn the generality of readers that this present book will seem to them only a rather more revolting mass of wordy nonsense than the last. . . .

Sixty pages farther on, unpacking his heart against universal education (which had after all given itself away by spawning the readers who had found the earlier essay a "revolting mass of wordy nonsense"), Lawrence thunders that "ideas" are "the most dangerous germs mankind has ever been injected with"; but the *idea* of "ideas" starts to penetrate the murk of his panic, the wordy nonsense thins a little, and out of it all at last, for a moment, emerges the Lawrence we stay up late for:

> The idea, the actual idea, must rise ever fresh, ever displaced, like the leaves of a tree, from out of the quickness of the sap. . . . The tree of life is a gay kind of tree that is forever dropping its leaves and budding out afresh quite different ones. If the last lot were thistle leaves, the next lot may be vine. You can never tell with the tree of life.

Ideas, according to this exquisite little tree-aria, aren't good or bad (as old Leo or D. H. Rananim insists they are), they're growing or shed, live or dead.

Lawrence had at least half a claim on the phoenix-emblem he chose for himself: nothing could quite keep him in sackcloth and ashes. One of his books during the same period was *Sea and Sardinia*, which he wrote in six weeks, having taken no notes, after a week's visit to Sardinia from Sicily. The book has his only extensive non-fictional representation of Frieda ("the queen bee" or "q-b"), direct, unintimidated, enthusiastic, not without misgivings—

> "I like it! I like it!" cries the q-b.
> "But could you live here?" She would like to say yes, but daren't.

—and a detailed account of their winter journey through desolate landscapes in cold and damp, in general discomfort, with wretched food and minimal conveniences: one of the fine comic scenes in Lawrence is the description of his hiking about the hills in a fury at the primitive sanitary arrangements of the inhabitants of the village of Sorgono—

> And the q-b was angry with me for my fury.
> "Why are you so indignant! Anyone would think your moral self had been outraged! Why take it morally? You petrify that man at the inn by the very way you speak to him, *such* condemnation! Why don't you take it as it comes? It's all life."
> But no, my rage is black, black, black. Why, heaven knows. But I think it was because Sorgono had seemed so fascinating to me, when I imagined it beforehand. Oh, so fascinating! If I had expected nothing I should not have been so hit. Blessed is he that expecteth nothing for he shall not be disappointed.
> I cursed the degenerate aborigines, the dirty-breasted host who *dared* to keep such an inn, the sordid villagers who had the baseness to squat their beastly human nastiness in this upland valley. All my praise of the long stocking-cap—you remember? —vanished from my mouth. I cursed them all, and the q-b for an interfering female. . . .

(but, back at the inn, the host takes a candle and leads them to the "stanza," the bare common-room, where "it was pitch-dark—but suddenly I saw a big fire of oak-root, a brilliant flamy, rich fire, and my rage in that second disappeared"); and not a Baedeker "sight" to be seen ("Sights are an irritating bore") and no companions except everybody they met on the way, as among the group by the fireplace in Sorgono, all in hats and overcoats, talking while a whole kid is being roasted over the fire:

"Signora!" said the girovago [wandering peddler]. "Do you understand Sardinian?"

"I understand Italian—and some Sardinian," she replied rather hotly. "And I know that you are trying to laugh at us— to make fun of us."

He laughed fatly and comfortably.

"Ah, Signora," he said. "We have a language that you wouldn't understand—not one word. . . ."

He leaned up to me, laughing.

"It is the language we use when the women are buying things and we don't want them to know what we say: me and him—"

"Oh," said I. "I know. We have that language in England. It is called thieves' Latin—*Latino dei furbi.*"

The men at the back suddenly laughed, glad to turn the joke against the forward girovago. He looked down his nose at me. But seeing I was laughing without malice, he leaned to me and said softly, secretly:

"What is your affair then? What affair is it, yours?"

"How? What?" I exclaimed, not understanding.

"*Che genere di affari?* What sort of business?"

"How—*affari?*" said I, still not grasping.

"What do you *sell?*" he said, flatly and rather spitefully. "What goods?"

"I don't sell anything," replied I, laughing to think he took us for some sort of strolling quacks or commercial travellers.

"Cloth—or something," he said cajolingly, slyly, as if to worm my secret out of me.

"But nothing at all. Nothing at all," said I. "We have come to Sardinia to see the peasant costumes—" I thought that might sound satisfactory.

"Ah, the costumes!" he said, evidently thinking I was a deep one. . . .

The Lawrences weren't tourists, and Lawrence was always at his best with people who didn't know who he was, where he could walk right in and talk and watch without feeling obliged to make pronouncements on the instant; talking and listening and getting angry (" 'You who look for dirty women,' say I, 'find dirty women everywhere' "), observing the religious procession that inspires a characteristic ode on women's clothes—

> . . . little girl-children with long skirts of scarlet cloth down to their feet, green-banded near the bottom: with white aprons bordered with vivid green and mingled colour: having little scarlet, purple-bound, open boleros over the full white shirts: and black head-cloths folded across their little chins, just leaving the lips clear, the face framed in black. Wonderful little girl-children, perfect and demure in the stiffish, brilliant costume, with black head-dress! Stiff as Velasquez princesses! . . .

(whereas the men have "hard, dangerous thighs" or "close breeches on their compact thighs"), toy-size donkeys as beasts of burden on the road, maskers in drag marching like marionettes in the street, a man playing a desperate game with a dog and a piece of bread, a little boy gazing wonderingly upward at the source of the slop-water that has splashed him, a little girl being sick while her parents don't bother to look sympathetic ("Sympathy would only complicate matters, and spoil that strange, remote virginal quality. The q-b says it is largely stupidity"), the "brisk and defiant" peasant women of Sardinia, the fellow-passenger's wife running along the platform with a "wild shriek, 'Madonna!' " as she is left behind by the train—

> The poor fat husband has been all the time on the little outside platform at the end of the carriage, holding out his hand to her and shouting frenzied scolding to her and frenzied yells for the train to stop. And the train has not stopped. And she is left —left on that God-forsaken station in the waning light.
>
> So, his face all bright, his eyes round and bright as two stars, absolutely transfigured by dismay, chagrin, anger and distress, he comes and sits in his seat, ablaze, stiff, speechless. . . .

—and the ship's old wood ("the paint wore away long ago"), "old oaken wood, so sea-fibred . . . so sound, so beautiful . . . rustless, life-born, living-tissued old wood: rustless as flesh is rustless."

Seven years later, doing what Moore homogenizes under the term "the thinned, satiric writing . . . of that last period,"

Lawrence sums up the "pa-assion" of *The Forsyte Saga* (with a "doggy" image he had tried and failed to manage a year or so earlier in *Lady Chatterley's Lover*):

> Mr. Galsworthy's treatment of passion is really rather shameful. The whole thing is doggy to a degree. The man has a temporary "hunger"; he is "on the heat" as they say of dogs. The heat passes. It's done. Trot away, if you're not tangled. Trot off, looking shamefacedly over your shoulder. People have been watching! Damn them! But never mind, it'll blow over. Thank God, the bitch is trotting in the other direction. She'll soon have another trail of dogs after her. That'll wipe out my traces. Good for that! Next time I'll get properly married and do my doggishness in my own house.

A year after wiping up Galsworthy (and less than a year to go), he expresses his polite stupefaction at the young English painter who has just said to him, "You do agree, don't you, that technically we know about all there is to know about painting?":

> I looked at him in amazement. It was obvious that a new-born babe was as fit to paint pictures as he was. He knew technically all there was to know about pictures: all about two-dimensional and three-dimensional composition, also the colour-dimension and the dimension of values in that view of composition which exists apart from form: all about the value of planes, the value of the angle in planes, the different values of the same colour on different planes: all about edges, visible edges, tangible edges, intangible edges: all about the nodality of form-groups, the constellating of mass-centres: all about the relativity of mass, the gravitation and the centrifugal force of masses, the resultant of the complex impinging of masses, the isolation of a mass in the line of vision: all about pattern, line pattern, edge pattern, tone pattern, colour pattern, and the pattern of moving planes: all about texture, impasto, surface, and what happens at the edge of the canvas: also which is the aesthetic centre of the canvas, the dynamic centre, the effulgent centre, the kinetic centre, the mathematical centre, and the Chinese centre: also the points of departure in the foreground, and the points of disappearance in the background, together with the various routes between these points, namely, as the crow flies, as the cow walks, as the mind intoxicated with

knowledge reels and gets there: all about spotting, what you spot, which spot, on the spot, how many spots, balance of spots, recedence of spots, spots on the explosive and spots on the co-ordinative vision: all about literary interest and how to hide it successfully from the policeman: all about photographic re-presentation . . .

—and much more.[5] Some critics give stock-market quotations (sometimes exact and eternal), some give advice to young writers on the doggy trail of technique ("Don't say 'dim lands of peace' "), some deliver formal orations on the passing of culture, community, and the Church Universal. Lawrence writes out of the fullness and relish of his curiosity about creatures and created things, whether he likes them or not (more often he writes about those he likes—Cooper, Verga, Hemingway—though he will scribble away eagerly about any book that comes to hand), as if he can never have enough of them.

Lawrence was once a little tiny boy in a mining village in England, who preferred playing with girls and whom the boys made fun of—

> Dicky Dicky Denches
> Plays with the wenches

—whom his mother loved (and who loved his mother) not wise-

---

[5]*Anna Karenina* may still have been ringing in Lawrence's ears. "[Mikhailov] . . . often heard the word 'technique' and could never understand what was meant by it. He knew it was supposed to mean a mechanical ability to paint and draw quite independent of the subject-matter. He had often noticed, as now when his picture was being praised, that technique was contrasted with inner quality, as though it were possible to paint well something that was bad." Certainly Lawrence remembered Mikhailov when he was writing Ursula's definitive riposte to Loerke in *Women in Love:*
> Loerke snorted with rage.
> "A picture of myself!" he repeated in derision. "Wissen sie, gnädige Frau, that is a Kunstwerk, a work of art. It is a work of art, it is a picture of nothing, of absolutely nothing. It has nothing to do with anything but itself. . . ."
> Ursula . . . was furious. . . .
> "It isn't a word of it true, of all this harangue you have made me," she replied flatly. "The horse is a picture of your own stock, stupid brutality, and the girl was a girl you loved and tortured and then ignored."
Mikhailov and Ursula would have been struck by Moore's critical term "prose."

ly but too well; a frail boy who early almost died of pneumonia and had "bronchial" illnesses for the rest of his life; read everything; fell in love first with a spiritual girl who exalted and balked and puzzled him, later with a physical woman who seemed to rescue him for the work he was destined to do.

Barely out of his 'teens he had begun writing the best short stories in English. In "The White Stocking," written when he was twenty-one, his powers are already manifest, especially his power to represent the intensity, momentariness, wariness, touchiness, unreliability of feeling, the very dance of feeling—

> The dance was over. Adams was detained. Elsie found herself beside Whiston. There was something shapely about him as he sat, about his knees and his distinct figure, that she clung to. It was as if he had enduring form. She put her hand on his knee. . . .
> "You don't want to be too free with Sam Adams," said Whiston cautiously, suffering. "You know what he is."
> "How, free?" she asked.
> "Why—you don't want to have too much to do with him."
> She sat silent. He was forcing her into consciousness of her position. But he could not get hold of her feelings, to change them. She had a curious, perverse desire that he should not.
> "I like him," she said.
> "What do you find to like in him?" he said, with a hot heart.
> "I don't know—but I like him," she said.
> She was immutable. He sat feeling heavy and dulled with rage. He was not clear as to what he felt. He sat there unliving whilst she danced. And she, distracted, lost to herself between the opposing forces of the two men, drifted. . . .

—not the fixed directions and grossly signaled changes of direction that fiction teaches us, despite our own experience, to regard as feeling, but how it *feels* to feel. For readers impressed by that waxworks nonpareil "The Dead," Lawrence's "The Shadow in the Rose Garden" is also about a man fighting a losing battle for his wife with the ghost of her former lover, but this one a crisp and downright account in which, though things get troubled and very disagreeable, yet nothing is settled and something remains possible (if only lifelong recrimination) and not a flake of symbolic snow falls anywhere in either of the British Isles. The elite list could be extended to a dozen or so: among them, "Tickets, Please," "New Eve and Old Adam" (a fictional go at Frieda, and Lawrence isn't so friendly as in *Sea and Sardinia*), "The Prussian Officer," "The Horse-Dealer's Daughter," "Samson and Delilah."

Ford Madox Ford, who "discovered" Lawrence for *The English Review*, used to say that everybody has a novel in him (though Ford, busily turning out a French novel or a James novel or a Conrad novel, never took the time to write his own). *Sons and Lovers* is Lawrence's novel: an astonishing piece of luck for posterity that at just this moment he had written enough fiction, and was free enough of his dead mother and of Jessie Chambers, and happy enough honeymooning with Frieda, and confident enough of his powers and his future, to make the truest statement in English about family life, mother-love, growing up, "lad-and-girl love," death in the family, staying alive.

He had read the Russians, and now he began writing a novel that eventually split into *The Rainbow* and *Women in Love* (he called it *The Sisters*, and at first thought of it as a pot-boiler!); he began to understand, with an eye on the Russians, that he could do something new in English fiction. The great Russians wrote novels about living souls and dying generations (they knew social types and drawing-rooms and ball-rooms nearly as well as Jane Austen did, but they had grander ambitions), about women who didn't merely wait for the right man, about conflicts for which society hadn't yet provided rules or solutions (Lawrence had of course read Hardy, who could be a resource in such matters but was small-scale by comparison with the Russians). In that famous letter to Edward Garnett, Lawrence trotted out a rocking-horse named Futurism-carbon-allotrope-diamond, whereupon Moore and all the other rocking-horse winners climbed into the saddle and rocked; but the real horse was locked away, as Logan Speirs suggests, in the Russian stables.

"Look! we have come through!" Lawrence exulted in a book of poems about the triumphant beginning of his marriage

("They may have come through," grumped the disaffected Bertrand Russell, no longer a candidate for Rananim, "but I don't see why I should look"); but feelings are unreliable, they spring up from nowhere, they revive, and "a man can no more slay a living desire in him, than he can prevent his body from feeling heat and cold." Lawrence completed *The Rainbow* in joyful confidence; two years later completed *Women in Love* in the stubborn need to finish something important he no longer quite believed in—not only this novel but his capacity as a novelist. He could neither slay his living desires nor say them out (as after *Anna Karenina* Tolstoy, unable to slay his living desires, resolved to spend the rest of his life denouncing them), and so (like Tolstoy) he lost access to the sources of his fiction. He became a novelist in name only, he wrote about other people, about everything (except himself) that interested him, about himself as a more or less public figure, about books and places with journalistic insouciance and speed, and he became in fact a writer.

Writing flourished everywhere in the nineteenth century; but if one considers the uniqueness and force, the unspecialized authority, of literature, the only writer of the nineteenth century was Tolstoy. In this century too, there have been poets, novelists, tale-tellers, essayists, critics, even, God help us! men of letters; but so far the only writer of the century—and there's very little time left—is Lawrence.

ⅡⅡ。
Jane Austen

The case against Jane Austen never quite blows away. It was drawn up in 1850 by Charlotte Brontë, who thought *Pride and Prejudice* "an accurate daguerrotyped portrait of a commonplace face" and Jane Austen a monster of prudence: "the Passions are perfectly unknown to her. . . . Jane Austen was a complete and most sensible lady, but a very incomplete, and rather insensible (*not senseless*) woman."[1] Almost a century passed before the case got stated with whole-hearted exasperation: "this old maid," snarled D. H. Lawrence, ". . . is, to my feeling, thoroughly unpleasant, English in the bad, mean, snobbish sense of the word"[2] (ranked patterns of correctness obliviously sitting out the Industrial Revolution and the Napoleonic wars); though even devotees come round to wondering, sooner or later, how far her example announced and legitimized and perhaps predetermined that imperturbable conspiracy of prudence, the nineteenth-century English novel. Can we forgive her? Angus Wilson doesn't: deplores that cautionary and provincial conspiracy and the writer he holds responsible

---

[1] *The Brontës: Their Friendships, Lives, and Correspondence,* eds. T.J. Wise and J.A. Symington (Oxford, 1932), Vol. III, p. 99.

[2] *A Propos of Lady Chatterley's Lover* (London, 1930), p. 58.

for it; taxes "Anglo-Saxon critics" with keeping Jane Austen's reputation artificially high; suavely taxes them with uniting in a conspiracy of their own, tight little islanders,

> . . . to canonize the foundress of the religion of the English novel, meaning by that religion a regard for all the qualities which the English novel does not share with the great novels of other countries. Not that I should care to deny the justification of this canonization, for through Jane Austen was transmitted to her English heirs Richardson's brilliant Grandisonian care for minutiae and mistrust of worldliness; while foreigners preferred Clarissa, Lovelace and passion; to be fair to the English tradition, the loss, I should say, was only a shade less theirs than ours. . . .[3]

Jane Austen is, then, practical, prosaic, prissy, and over-rated. Wilson seems to be saying that, overrated as she is, she nonetheless somehow managed to impose her personal and artistic shortcomings on three or four generations of English novelists ("the English tradition": i.e., Dickens, Trollope, Hardy, Lawrence, *et al.*) as well as (why stop now?) on the world they lived in and wrote about—an imputation which, if true, would make her the most influential artistic second-rater in history. But Jane Austen might be as superb as some think she is and she would still have had no power to retard or deflect or, for that matter, accelerate the rise of the middle class. Victorianism preceded Queen Victoria; in 1821 Sir Walter Scott used a family anecdote to illustrate a moral change that had been going on over the previous sixty years and more (the period included Jane Austen's entire lifetime)—a massive and irresistible ossifying of inhibitions against explicitness:

---

[3]"The Neighbourhood of Tombuctoo," in *Critical Essays on Jane Austen,* ed. B.C. Southam (London, 1968), p. 185. But Continental writers adored *both* Richardsons: e.g., in "The Portrait" (1841-2), Gogol eulogizes "Prince R., one of the best and most honourable of all young noblemen of that time, handsome of face and of a noble, chivalrous character, the ideal hero of novels and women, a Grandison in every respect." *The Overcoat and Other Tales of Good and Evil*, tr. David Magarshack (New York, 1965), p. 145.

It is very difficult to answer your Ladyship's curious question concerning change of taste; but whether in young or old, it takes place insensibly without the parties being aware of it. A grand-aunt of my own, Mrs Keith of Ravelstone, who was a person of some condition, being a daughter of Sir John Swinton of Swinton—lived with unabated vigour of intellect to a very advanced age. She was very fond of reading, and enjoyed it to the last of her long life. One day she asked me, when we happened to be alone together, whether I had ever seen Mrs Behn's novels?—I confessed the charge.—Whether I could get her a sight of them. —I said with some hesitation, I believed I could; but that I did not think she would like either the manners, or the language, which approached too near that of Charles II.'s time to be quite proper reading. 'Nevertheless,' said the good old lady, 'I remember them being so much admired, and being so much interested in them myself, that I wish to look at them again.' To hear was to obey. So I sent Mrs Aphra Behn, curiously sealed up, with 'private and confidential' on the packet, to my gay old grand-aunt. The next time I saw her afterwards, she gave me back Aphra, properly wrapped up, with nearly these words:— 'Take back your bonny Mrs Behn; and, if you will take my advice, put her in the fire, for I found it impossible to get through the very first novel. But is it not,' she said, 'a very odd thing that I, an old woman of eighty and upwards, sitting alone, feel myself ashamed to read a book which, sixty years ago, I have heard read aloud for the amusement of large circles, consisting of the first and most creditable society in London.'

"This, of course," Scott concluded with a smugness that sets off all the more distinctly his beautiful picture of the alert, troubled, and philosophical old gentlewoman, "was owing to the gradual improvement of the national taste and delicacy."[4]

Jane Austen wasn't responsible for the Industrial Revolution or the Albert Memorial. As to "the gradual improvement of the national taste and delicacy," so far was she from being responsible for it that, by the time she began writing her novels, it had very nearly finished off the residue of eighteenth-century candor in Jane Austen and everybody else writing

---

[4]J.G. Lockhart, *Memoirs of the Life of Sir Walter Scott, Bart.*, Second Edition (Edinburgh and London, 1839), Vol. VI, pp. 406-7.

books: her *juvenilia* (1790-3) can still be cheekily receptive to drunkenness, thievery, adultery, illegitimacy; by the date of *Northanger Abbey* (c. 1803), John Thorpe is barely allowed to swear with a tactful dash ("oh, d— it!"); in *Sense and Sensibility* (revised and published in 1811), Marianne can still exclaim "Good God!" fully spelled out and remain a lady; but none of Jane Austen's characters will ever after venture to take such liberties. Sixty years earlier, young Mrs. Keith of Ravelstone had listened comfortably while Aphra Behn's novels were being read aloud in a respectable drawing-room, and Richardson (in *Clarissa*, 1748) hadn't scrupled to transcribe for posterity Lovelace's explicit appraisal of the "neatness" and "elegance" of the "dairy-works" of the widow Sorlings' two pretty daughters.

So if Jane Austen doesn't have as liberal a vocabulary as Richardson, Sterne, Fielding, Smollett, neither will Dickens or George Eliot or any of the Brontës and for the same reasons. Exactly, says Wilson, that's why English novelists of the nineteenth century are inferior to the French and Russian, who, making off across the Channel with "Clarissa, Lovelace and passion," leave to English fiction Richardson's less valuable legacy, the "Grandisonian care for minutiae and mistrust of worldliness." Charlotte Brontë, on the other hand, sister of Emily and author of *Jane Eyre*, is in no position to concede the Continental monopoly of passion. Jane Austen lacks it no doubt ("the Passions are perfectly unknown to her"); but not every nineteenth-century English novelist or her sister is deficient in men on horseback, nubile governesses,[5] depressing scenery, locks and bolts, occasional moderate to heavy rain, gigantic tantrums, *rigor mortis* (bite-me-to-death-I-love-it) *à la* Heathcliff: "I tried to close his eyes. . . . They would not shut: they seemed to sneer at my attempts, and his parted lips and sharp white teeth sneered too!"—if only, cried Herbert Read

---

[5]Regarding passion and *Jane Eyre*, Lawrence (cross-grained as ever) comments: "I don't think any married woman would have written [it]. . . . In [*Jane Eyre*] . . . there is a certain naive attitude to men which would hardly survive a year of married life." *Phoenix* (New York, 1968) p. 337.

quoting the passage, if only Jane Austen could have felt and written like *that*![6] After all, Mrs. Bennet assures Darcy, "there is quite as much of *that* going on in the country [not only the Brontës' Yorkshire but the Austens' Hampshire] as in town." The case against Jane Austen always comes down, with slightly averted eyes, to country matters. What both Angus Wilson and Charlotte Brontë mean by passion, singular or plural, is sexuality, particularly the sexuality of women; the sexual precedence of women: erotic excitability and readiness (with the right partner, naturally), an eagerness for physical connection (sanctioned by love, it goes without saying), a desire and capacity for orgasm; coitus as the warmth of life.

Certainly *Clarissa* is, as Wilson suggests (lamenting its abduction by foreigners), the source and text. Richardson had already, with *Pamela*, made a false start by inventing the woman's novel or modern romance, in which the heroine sacrifices everything for the sake of a lifetime of unbounded self-satisfaction. With *Clarissa* however, as its earliest readers recognized at once, Richardson invented a new kind of adventure story—translated to the Continent, it turned into the modern novel—in which the heroine comes forward at last to take her chances and the subject is passion. Lovelace, archaic male, keeps imagining himself as the hero of an old-fashioned novel and Clarissa as his goal or prey; keeps so frantically busy playing Don Juan or the Marquis de Sade or Heathcliff or Rochester or Quetzalcoatl that, in a novel twice the length of *War and Peace*, he never notices Clarissa's unintimidated passion and readiness; and his distraction finally wrecks them both.

Clarissa is pristine and unique, but at least one of Jane Austen's women might have done almost as well as Clarissa captivating Lovelace and giving him fits: Marianne Dashwood. The anti-Austenites don't help their case when they fail to acknowledge that Marianne is an obvious exception to it. Indeed, as they might argue, *Sense and Sensibility* is itself an exception, a runaway great novel (like *Madame Bovary*) whose fussy moral scheme isn't proof against this or that intransigent

---

[6]*English Prose Style* (Boston, 1955), pp. 109-112.

character—an Emma Bovary or a Marianne Dashwood, for example. The first published novel "By a Lady" (as the title page designated the author) who was one of the two spinster daughters of a rural clergyman, *Sense and Sensibility* is paved with good intentions: in her public debut the author intends to avoid all risks, even with the title itself, which therefore proves to be not an ironic balancing-act (like the title of her second novel, *Pride and Prejudice*) but a raw *a priori* judgment. Sense is right and sensibility is wrong: so she insists from the outset, as early as the scenes introducing Elinor and Marianne. The author proposes that sensibility (passion, flightiness, irrationality) has charms, but sense (prudence, keeping the lid on, calculating the odds) pays off; she is determined to prove what nobody ever doubted. Only, already in Chapter II, the moral scheme gets scrambled quite a bit by those exhilarating flint-hearted philistines Mr. and Mrs. John Dashwood, whose talent for reciprocal rationalization proves that though sense is shrewder than sensibility it's crazier too. What the novel goes on to prove beyond a doubt, over the author's protests, is that sense (not only the John Dashwoods' but Elinor's) is mean and deadly, but sensibility—i.e., Marianne—is generous, responsive, frank, loyal, loving, passionate, tragically open to the torment of rejected love:

> At that moment she first perceived him, and her whole countenance glowing with sudden delight, she would have moved towards him instantly, had not her sister caught hold of her.
>
> "Good heavens!" she exclaimed, "he is there—he is there —Oh! why does he not look at me? why cannot I speak to him?"
>
> "Pray, pray be composed," cried Elinor, "and do not betray what you feel to every body present. Perhaps he has not observed you yet."
>
> This however was more than she could believe herself; and to be composed at such a moment was not only beyond the reach of Marianne, it was beyond her wish. She sat in an agony of impatience, which affected every feature.
>
> At last he turned round again, and regarded them both; she started up, and pronouncing his name in a tone of affection, held out her hand to him. He approached, and addressing him-

self rather to Elinor than Marianne, as if wishing to avoid her eye, and determined not to observe her attitude, inquired in a hurried manner after Mrs. Dashwood, and asked how long they had been in town. Elinor was robbed of all presence of mind by such an address, and was unable to say a word. But the feelings of her sister were instantly expressed. Her face was crimsoned over, and she exclaimed in a voice of the greatest emotion, "Good God! Willoughby, what is the meaning of this? Have you not received my letters? Will you not shake hands with me?"

He could not then avoid it, but her touch seemed painful to him, and he held her hand only for a moment. During all this time he was evidently struggling for composure. Elinor watched his countenance and saw its expression becoming more tranquil. After a moment's pause, he spoke with calmness.

"I did myself the honour of calling in Berkeley-street last Tuesday, and very much regretted that I was not fortunate enough to find yourselves and Mrs. Jennings at home. My card was not lost, I hope."

"But have you not received my notes?" cried Marianne in the wildest anxiety. "Here is some mistake I am sure—some dreadful mistake. What can be the meaning of it? Tell me, Willoughby; for heaven's sake tell me, what is the matter?"

Nobody admired Jane Austen more intelligently than George Moore, and nobody has written better about this scene:

. . . the theme of the book is a disappointment in love. . . . We all know how terrible these disappointments are, and how they crush and break up life, for the moment reducing it to dust; the sufferer neither sees nor hears, but walks like a somnambulist through an empty world. So it is with Marianne, who cannot give up hope, and the Dashwoods go to London in search of the young man; and every attempt is made to recapture him, and every effort wrings her heart. She hears of him, but never sees him, till at last she perceives him in a back room, and at once, her whole countenance blazing forth with a sudden delight, she would have moved towards him instantly had not her sister laid her hand on her arm, and in the page and a half that follows Miss Austen gives us all the agony of passion the human heart can feel; she was the first; and none has written the scene that we all desire to write as truthfully as she has; when

Balzac and Tourguéneff rewrote it they wrote more elaborately, but their achievements are not greater. In Miss Austen the means are as simple as the result is amazing. Listen to it again. A young girl of twenty, jilted, comes up to London with her mother and sister, and she sees her lover at an assembly; he comes forward and addresses a few words more to her sister than to herself within hearing of a dozen people, and it is here that we find the burning human heart in English prose narrative for the first, and, alas, for the last time.[7]

Moore and Angus Wilson remind us of a fact of literary history, that the French and Russian novelists took up passion from English fiction and carried it off for their own purposes; but Moore contends also that the only English novelist in whose work (in only one of whose novels, rather) they could have found the literary model of passion was not Richardson, but Jane Austen! The notion, however historically unsound (and unfair to her later novels, which Moore admits not having read lately), begins to seem less fantastic when Moore describes what he considers Jane Austen's great and fundamental discovery:

> . . . it was Miss Austen's spinsterhood that allowed her to discover the Venusberg in the modern drawing-room. . . . We do not go into society for the pleasure of conversation, but for the pleasure of sex, direct or indirect. Everything is arranged for this end: the dresses, the dances, the food, the wine, the music! Of this truth we are all conscious now, but should we have discovered it without Miss Austen's help? It was certainly she who perceived it, and her books are permeated with it, just as Wordsworth's poems are with a sense of deity in nature; and is it not this deep instinctive knowledge that makes her drawing-rooms seem more real than anybody else's? Marianne loves beyond Juliet's or Isolde's power; and our wonder at her passion is heightened by the fact that it wears out in drawing-rooms among chaperons. . . .[8]

Richardson's Venusberg is a London brothel or a remote country-house (only the lovers are real). Jane Austen's is her

[7]*Avowals* (London, 1924), pp. 39-40.

[8]*Ibid.*, pp. 57-8.

own familiar drawing-room, which "seem[s] more real than
anybody else's" because the unregarded and attentive spinster,[9]
lacking other diversions, observes what's really going on there
—especially *that*, as Mrs. Bennet would say:

> "You begin to comprehend me, do you?" cried . . . [Bing-
> ley], turning towards . . . [Elizabeth].
> "Oh! yes—I understand you perfectly."
> "I wish I might take this for a compliment; but to be so
> easily seen through I am afraid is pitiful."
> "That is as it happens. It does not necessarily follow that a
> deep, intricate character is more or less estimable than such a
> one as yours."
> "Lizzy," cried her mother, "remember where you are, and
> do not run on in the wild manner that you are suffered to do at
> home."
> "I did not know before," continued Bingley immediately,
> "that you were a studier of character. It must be an amusing
> study."
> "Yes; but intricate characters are the *most* amusing. They
> have at least that advantage."
> "The country," said Darcy, "can in general supply but few
> subjects for such a study. In a country neighborhood you move
> in a very confined and unvarying society."
> "But people themselves alter so much, that there is some-
> thing new to be observed in them for ever."
> "Yes, indeed," cried Mrs. Bennet, offended by his manner

---

[9]Making allowances for the dash of vitriol, Mary Russell Mitford's contemporary gossiping gives us an impression of the effect Jane Austen must have
had on her neighbors once they knew exactly who was sitting there: ". . . a
friend of mine, who visits her now, says that she has stiffened into the most
perpendicular, precise, taciturn piece of 'single blessedness' that ever existed,
and that, till *Pride and Prejudice* showed what a precious gem was hidden in
that unbending case, she was no more regarded in society than a poker or a
fire-screen, or any other thin upright piece of wood or iron that fills its corner in peace and quietness. The case is very different now; she is still a poker—
but a poker of whom every one is afraid. It must be confessed that this silent
observation from such an observer is rather formidable . . . a wit, a delineator
of character, who does not talk, is terrific indeed!" R.B. Johnson (ed.), *The
Letters of Mary Russell Mitford* (New York, 1925), p. 127 (Letter to Sir William Elford, April 3, 1815).

of mentioning a country neighbourhood. "I assure you there is quite as much of *that* going on in the country as in town."

Every body was surprised; and Darcy, after looking at her for a moment, turned silently away. . . .

Everybody in this allegory of love, from Ungovernable Indelicacy to Scrupulous Correction, knows that winning is everything; but only those who win know how many different ways there are to lose:

Mrs. Bennet, who fancied she had gained a complete victory over him, continued her triumph.

"I cannot see that London has any great advantage over the country for my part, except the shops and public places. The country is a vast deal pleasanter, is not it, Mr. Bingley?"

"When I am in the country," he replied, "I never wish to leave it; and when I am in town it is pretty much the same. They have each their advantages, and I can be equally happy in either."

"Aye—that is because you have the right disposition. But that gentleman," looking at Darcy, "seemed to think the country was nothing at all."

"Indeed, Mama, you are mistaken," said Elizabeth, blushing for her mother. "You quite mistook Mr. Darcy. He only meant that there were not such a variety of people to be met with in the country as in town, which you must acknowledge to be true."

"Certainly, my dear, nobody said there were; but as to not meeting with many people in this neighbourhood, I believe there are few neighbourhoods larger. I know we dine with four and twenty families."

Nothing but concern for Elizabeth could enable Bingley to keep his countenance. His sister was less delicate, and directed her eye towards Mr. Darcy with a very expressive smile. . . .

Elizabeth, the "studier of character," does in fact perfectly understand Bingley, who is a faultless and predictable young man and therefore of no further interest to her. Foolish, touchy Mrs. Bennet, still fascinated by country matters, knows very well what the drawing-room game is, and is indecorous enough to flaunt (if not actually name) what she knows. Bingley's sister knows that Mrs. Bennet is a loser, but doesn't know that only losers solicit praise for recognizing losers. Everybody goes back to square one except Elizabeth and Darcy:

> After playing some Italian songs, Miss Bingley varied the charm by a lively Scotch air; and soon afterwards Mr. Darcy, drawing near Elizabeth, said to her—
> "Do you not feel a great inclination, Miss Bennet, to seize such an opportunity of dancing a reel?"
> She smiled, but made no answer. He repeated the question, with some surprise at her silence.
> "Oh!" said she, "I heard you before; but I could not immediately determine what to say in reply. You wanted me, I know, to say 'Yes,' that you might have the pleasure of despising my taste; but I always delight in overthrowing those kind of schemes, and cheating a person of their premeditated contempt. I have therefore made up my mind to tell you, that I do not want to dance a reel at all—and now despise me if you dare."
> "Indeed I do not dare."
> Elizabeth, having rather expected to affront him, was amazed at his gallantry; but there was a mixture of sweetness and archness in her manner which made it difficult for her to affront anybody; and Darcy had never been so bewitched by any woman as he was by her. He really believed, that were it not for the inferiority of her connections, he should be in some danger.

At first Darcy, like Lovelace too vain and masculine to know how to win by yielding, becomes merely passion's slave and blunders into the grotesque proposal that Elizabeth angrily rejects:

> ... when he ceased, the colour rose into her cheeks, and she said,
> "In such cases as this, it is, I believe, the established mode to express a sense of obligation for the sentiments avowed, however unequally they may be returned. It is natural that obligation should be felt, and if I could *feel* gratitude, I would now thank you. But I cannot—I have never desired your good opinion, and you have certainly bestowed it most unwillingly. I am sorry to have occasioned pain to any one. It has been most unconsciously done, however, and I hope will be of short duration. The feelings which, you tell me, have long prevented the acknowledgment of your regard, can have little difficulty in overcoming it after this explanation."

Mr. Darcy, who was leaning against the mantle-piece with his eyes fixed on her face, seemed to catch her words with no less resentment than surprise. His complexion became pale with anger, and the disturbance of his mind was visible in every feature. He was struggling for the appearance of composure, and would not open his lips, till he believed himself to have attained it. The pause was to Elizabeth's feelings dreadful. At length, in a voice of forced calmness, he said,

"And this is all the reply which I am to have the honour of expecting! I might, perhaps, wish to be informed why, with so little *endeavour* at civility, I am thus rejected. But it is of small importance."

It's a remarkable scene, in its furiously formal Johnsonian cadences it tells more about love and marriage and the sex war than we could learn from a secret diary or any number of Brontë manuals:

"I might as well enquire," replied she, "why with so evident a design of offending and insulting me, you chose to tell me that you liked me against your will, against your reason, and even against your character? Was not this some excuse for incivility, if I *was* uncivil? But I have other provocations. You know I have. Had not my own feelings decided against you, had they been indifferent, or had they even been favourable, do you think that any consideration would tempt me to accept the man, who has been the means of ruining, perhaps for ever, the happiness of a most beloved sister?" . . .

She paused, and saw with no slight indignation that he was listening with an air which proved him wholly unmoved by any feeling of remorse. He even looked at her with a smile of affected incredulity.

"Can you deny that you have done it?" she repeated.

With assumed tranquillity he then replied, "I have no wish of denying that I did every thing in my power to separate my friend from your sister, or that I rejoice in my success. Towards *him* I have been kinder than towards myself."

Trying to sympathize with Charlotte Brontë, one can imagine why it would never have occurred to her that Elizabeth and Darcy are *roused* to this pitch of formal rhetoric; one can imagine why such a refinement and dramatization of the John-

sonian idiom would seem as mechanical and unexpressive to an
impatient nineteenth-century sensibility as, say, Dr. Johnson
himself seemed to Wordsworth and Coleridge. Surely what
bothers her is Elizabeth's (Jane Austen's) full and unapologetic
articulateness: woman's province is feeling, and feeling ought
to be inarticulate or at least convulsive and incoherent. But—
like all of Jane Austen's other heroines (except those hole-and-
corner anomalies, Elinor Dashwood and Fanny Price)—
Elizabeth is as strong and brave in her talk as in her feeling.
How else could she ever penetrate to the quick of an armored
male ego like Darcy's? In *Mansfield Park* Mary Crawford,
baffled by a comparable male ego, drops decorum altogether
and goes so far as to transform Jane Austen's drawing-room
into a boudoir (the speaker is poor beleaguered Edmund):

". . . I had gone a few steps, Fanny, when I heard the door
open behind me. 'Mr. Bertram,' said she. I looked back. 'Mr.
Bertram,' said she, with a smile—but it was a smile ill-suited to
the conversation that had passed, a saucy playful smile, seeming
to invite, in order to subdue me; at least, it appeared so to me. I
resisted; it was the impulse of the moment to resist, and still
walked on. I have since—sometimes—for a moment—regretted
that I did not go back; but I know I was right. . . ."

Mary is a century too early, and the author can't approve; but
Elizabeth and Marianne and Catherine Morland and Emma
Woodhouse would all of them have understood Mary's last
choice and Edmund's lingering regret.

So, of course, would Anne Elliot. Can Charlotte Brontë or
Angus Wilson or D. H. Lawrence have read *Persuasion*? (Herbert Read seems to have read it, because he cites the scene of
Louisa's fall from the Cobb as evidence of the marionette-like
unnaturalness of Jane Austen's characters.[10]) Suppose Charlotte Brontë, coming on the scene a generation earlier, had
stated not in 1850 but in 1813 her reservations about the author
of *Pride and Prejudice*, and Jane Austen had heard them and
come to a decision: Well, if this literary lady considers Elizabeth or me (not to mention Marianne) such a cold fish, maybe

---

[10]*Loc. cit.*

I'd better invent a heroine who's warm enough for absolutely anybody—I'll invent Anne Elliot, of course. For instance, since Miss Brontë calls me "a very incomplete, and rather insensible (*not senseless*) woman," I'll use "senseless" (minus italics, so she won't think I'm plagiarizing) as the very word to specify the kind of joy Anne feels at the moment when she can begin to hope again—

> No, it was not regret which made Anne's heart beat in spite of herself, and brought the colour into her cheeks when she thought of Captain Wentworth unshackled and free. She had some feelings which she was ashamed to investigate. They were too much like joy, senseless joy!

As far as I can (resolves the penitent author of *Pride and Prejudice*) I'll model her in anticipation after—Jane Eyre! except she'll be open-eyed, clear-headed, unsentimental—

> Anne had not wanted this visit to Uppercross, to learn that a removal from one set of people to another, though at a distance of only three miles, will often include a total change of conversation, opinion, and idea. She had never been staying there before, without being struck by it, or without wishing that other Elliots could have her advantage in seeing how unknown, or unconsidered there, were the affairs which at Kellynch-hall were treated as of such general publicity and pervading interest; yet, with all this experience, she believed she must now submit to feel that another lesson, in the art of knowing our own nothingness beyond our own circle, was becoming necessary for her. . . .

—and she'll be loving, large-hearted, ready for delight, a wellspring of good feeling—

> The Crofts . . . brought with them their country habit of being almost always together. He was ordered to walk, to keep off the gout, and Mrs. Croft seemed to go shares with him in every thing, and to walk for her life, to do him good. Anne saw them wherever she went. Lady Russell took her out in her carriage almost every morning, and she never failed to think of them, and never failed to see them. Knowing their feelings as she did, it was a most attractive picture of happiness to her. She always watched them as long as she could; delighted to fancy

she understood what they might be talking of, as they walked along in happy independence, or equally delighted to see the Admiral's hearty shake of the hand when he encountered an old friend, and observe their eagerness of conversation when occasionally forming into a little knot of the navy, Mrs. Croft looking as intelligent and keen as any of the officers around her.

—and she'll be intense, spontaneous, unpremeditatedly delight-ful—

. . . and Anne—but it would be an insult to the nature of Anne's felicity, to draw any comparison between it and her sister's; the origin of one all selfish vanity, of the other all generous attachment.

Anne saw nothing, thought nothing of the brilliancy of the room. Her happiness was from within. Her eyes were bright, and her cheeks glowed,—but she knew nothing about it. She was thinking only of the last half hour, and as they passed to their seats, her mind took a hasty range over it. His choice of subjects, his expressions, and still more his manner and look, had been such as she could see in only one light. . . .

Unlike Elizabeth or Marianne (thinks their creator, warmed to the task), Anne won't be much of a talker, I'll see to that; she'll be nearly as introspective as scruffy little Jane Eyre: in her daily concerns she'll be the helpful, unintrusive maiden aunt, nurse, confidante, companion, baby-sitter (I've done the whole routine myself); rather like a governess. But some readers just won't be fooled by the real thing, they'll keep holding out for the woman's-novel imitation.

For the real thing is sometimes almost too bare and pain-ful to contemplate: so Jane Austen showed with Marianne and now devotes an entire novel to showing moment by moment with Anne, as when Anne braces herself to survive her first meeting with Wentworth after seven years—

. . . a thousand feelings rushed on Anne, of which this was the most consoling, that it would soon be over. And it was soon over. In two minutes after Charles's preparation, the others appeared; they were in the drawing-room. Her eye half met Captain Wentworth's; a bow, a curtsey passed; she heard his voice —he talked to Mary, said all that was right; said something to the Miss Musgroves, enough to mark an easy footing: the room seemed full—full of persons and voices—but a few minutes ended it. Charles shewed himself at the window, all was ready, their visitor had bowed and was gone; the Miss Musgroves were gone too, suddenly resolving to walk to the end of the village with the sportsmen: the room was cleared, and Anne might finish her breakfast as she could.

"It is over! it is over!" she repeated to herself again, and again, in nervous gratitude. "The worst is over!"

It isn't over, but she might as well take a breath while thinking so. Too much depends on the mistake she made years ago and can't imagine she'll ever have the chance to make again. *Persuasion* is about loneliness and growing old gracefully; about lost and last chances; about staying out of the way, perfecting "the art of knowing our own nothingness"; and about passion, which covers with confusion, electrifies with senseless joy, stuns or transfixes or agitates—passion tried and true, which destroys the illusion of one's own insignificance and discloses as if on stone tablets the meaning of the past:

It was in one of these short meetings, each apparently occupied in admiring a fine display of green-house plants, that she said—

"I have been thinking over the past, and trying impartially to judge of the right and the wrong, I mean with regard to myself; and I must believe that I was right, much as I suffered from it, that I was perfectly right in being guided by the friend whom you will love better than you do now. To me, she was in the place of a parent. Do not mistake me, however. I am not saying that she did not err in her advice. It was, perhaps, one of those cases in which advice is good or bad only as the event decides; and for myself, I certainly never should, in any circumstance of tolerable similarity, give such advice. But I mean, that I was right in submitting to her, and that if I had done otherwise, I should have suffered more in continuing the engagement than I did even in giving it up, because I should have suffered in my conscience. I have now, as far as such a sentiment is allowable in human nature, nothing to reproach myself with; and if I mistake not, a strong sense of duty is no bad part of a woman's portion."

Anne, learning how to occupy space again, may be excused this slight case of conscience as she reclaims the past, especially when a moment later she replies with all possible colloquial alacrity to Wentworth's unnecessary question:

> ". . . Tell me if, when I returned to England in the year eight, with a few thousand pounds, and was posted into the Laconia, if I had then written to you, would you have answered my letter? would you, in short, have renewed the engagement then?"
>
> "Would I!" was all her answer; but the accent was decisive enough.

Women know what they know but—as Anne, newly free to speak out, is glad to be reminded by Captain Harville—it's men who write the books:

> ". . . Well, Miss Elliot, . . . we shall never agree I suppose upon this point. No man and woman would, probably. But let me observe that all histories are against you, all stories, prose and verse. If I had such a memory as Benwick, I could bring you fifty quotations in a moment on my side the argument, and I do not think I ever opened a book in my life which had not something to say upon woman's inconstancy. Songs and proverbs, all talk of woman's fickleness. But perhaps you will say, these were all written by men."
>
> "Perhaps I shall.—Yes, yes, if you please, no reference to examples in books. Men have had every advantage of us in telling their own story. Education has been theirs in so much higher a degree; the pen has been in their hands. I will not allow books to prove any thing."

Because (Anne almost says, glorying in her exemplary rôle) no book, until this one, has ever told the truth about *me*. Richardson could do the great incendiary talker, Clarissa; but it took Jane Austen, in her last novel, to do Anne Elliot, the great quiet incendiary, the unregarded lady in the drawing-room, who till she has all the reason in the world leaves the talking to others, questions no arrangements while noticing them all, never imposes, always assists, and keeps her heart and soul available for anybody—Captain Wentworth or the Crofts or the author or the reader—who might at some time or other have the good luck to accompany her on her unnoticed morning walk along the streets of Bath:

> Prettier musings of high-wrought love and eternal constancy, could never have passed along the streets of Bath, than Anne was sporting with from Camden-place to Westgate-buildings. It was almost enough to spread purification and perfume all the way.

IV.
Johnson

Johnson's reputation is deadly, and these volumes[1] of his essays and autobiographical fragments don't offer much evidence against it. Of all the great literary figures, he is in his own work the least read from mere curiosity and the most effectively mutilated by his academic keepers, who smack their lips over the soundness of the bullying old eccentric of the moral essays, quarantine Boswell with labels like "libidinous puppy" (along alleys, on deserted bridges, in boudoirs, even burning penitently with the clap, the young Scotsman couldn't get enough of London whores and actresses), and never blink at the unbridled despondencies with which the Christian Doctor stamps out any residual hopefulness in the utterly damnable human race:

> The depravity of mankind is so easily discoverable, that nothing but the desert or the cell can exclude it from notice. The knowledge of crimes intrudes uncalled and undesired. They whom their abstraction from common occurrences hinders from seeing iniquity, will quickly have their attention awakened by feeling it. Even he who ventures not into the world, may learn

[1] *The Yale Edition of the Works of Samuel Johnson*, Vol. I: *Diaries, Prayers, and Annals* (New Haven, 1958); Vol. II: *The Idler and the Adventurer* (New Haven, 1963); Vols. III, IV, V: *The Rambler* (New Haven, 1969).

its corruption in his closet. For what are treatises of morality, but persuasives to the practice of duties, for which no arguments would be necessary, but that we are continually tempted to violate or neglect them? What are all the records of history, but narratives of successive villanies, of treasons and usurpations, massacres and wars?

Though a pale ray may now and then penetrate his megrims, it hardly alters the atmosphere of exanimate platitude:

> That familiarity produces neglect, has been long observed. The effect of all external objects, however great or splendid, ceases with their novelty: the courtier stands without emotion in the royal presence; the rustic tramples under his foot the beauties of the spring, with little attention to their colour or their fragrance; and the inhabitant of the coast darts his eye upon the immense diffusion of waters, without awe, wonder, or terror.

—down, down to the lowest circle of bathos:

> That every day has its pains and sorrows is universally experienced, and almost universally confessed; but let us not attend only to mournful truths; if we look impartially about us we shall find that every day has likewise its pleasures and its joys.

If, really, we look impartially about us, nothing in "our present state" will serve. "Of riches," declares Johnson, "as of every thing else, the hope is more than the enjoyment" (one of the Rambler's or Idler's multitudinous generalizations on which "Speak for yourself" is the appropriate comment). Pleasure? there's nothing in it: "Such is . . . [its] emptiness . . . that we are always impatient of the present. Attainment is followed by neglect, and possession by disgust; and the malicious remark of the Greek epigrammatist on marriage may be applied to every other course of life, that its two days of happiness are the first and the last." Indeed he goes so far as to make a statement of such stunning ignorance that, even omitting to remind Johnson of the fact of laughter, the libidinous puppy or one of those obliging actresses could have corrected it any night in the world.:

> Pain is less subject than pleasure to caprices of expression. The torments of disease, and the grief for irremediable misfor-

tunes, sometimes are such as no words can declare, and can only be signified by groans, or sobs, or inarticulate ejaculations. Man has from nature a mode of utterance peculiar to pain, but he has none peculiar to pleasure, because he never has pleasure but in such degrees as the ordinary use of language may equal or surpass.

Sometimes the fear of the world (as well as, in this instance, a recollection of Swift) contracts into a strong metaphor:

It is well known, that, exposed to a microscope, the smoothest polish of the most solid bodies discovers cavities and prominences; and that the softest bloom of roseate virginity repels the eye with excrescences and discolorations. The perceptions as well as the senses may be improved to our own disquiet, and we may, by diligent cultivation of the powers of dislike, raise in time an artificial fastidiousness, which shall fill the imagination with phantoms of turpitude, shew us the naked skeleton of every delight, and present us only with the pains of pleasure, and the deformities of beauty.

And just once, unintentionally, the moralist's rhetoric of rejection knots itself up into an agonized indictment of a God whose only guarantee to mankind is posthumous:

It is scarcely to be imagined, that Infinite Benevolence would create a being capable of enjoying so much more than is here to be enjoyed, and qualified by nature to prolong pain by remembrance and anticipate it by terror, if he was not designed for something nobler and better than a state, in which many of his faculties can serve only for his torment, in which he is to be importuned by desires that never can be satisfied, to feel many evils which he had no power to avoid, and to fear many which he shall never feel: there will surely come a time, when every capacity of happiness shall be filled, and none shall be wretched but by his own fault.

Boswell calls him "The Sage"; but impersonal judiciousness, sustained and moderate reflection, prudence and resource with their comfortable aphorisms (à la his remarkably different transatlantic contemporary, Benjamin Franklin), Christian or at least stoic submissiveness to the will of God and the nature of things—all the traits answerable to what the Enlightenment, of which Johnson was England's most illustrious representative, identified as wisdom—are in neither his character nor his writing. No renunciatory and expiatory metaphysic is large enough for him; he suffers pain and terror unrelieved by the consolations of philosophy; he is burdened, not as he thinks by the guilt and self-hatred whose pious names he borrows from the eighteenth-century remains of Christian dogma, but by the sense of unused capacity ("there will surely come a time, when every capacity of happiness shall be filled, and none shall be wretched but by his own fault"), the personal sense of waste and loss, the immoderateness of desire, the weight of his inapplicable talents and passions.

Johnson's preoccupation in the essays is not so much religious or moral as hydrostatic: his most personal imagery is less of sin and penance than of filling and killing time, of voids and the hope of repletion. "Such things . . . as other philosophers often attribute to various and contradictory causes," according to Mrs. Thrale, "appeared to him uniform enough; all was done to fill up the time. . . . One man, for example, was profligate and wild, as we call it, followed the girls, or sat still at the gaming-table. 'Why, life must be filled up (says Johnson), and the man who is not capable of intellectual pleasures must content himself with such as his senses can afford.' " A favorite word of Johnson's is "vacuity": about riches (as elsewhere about every other human concern), he remarks (in *The Idler* Number 73) that "we find them insufficient to fill up the vacuities of life." If Johnson were more religious or more moral, his essays would be considerably livelier. Nor is it his sesquipedalian propensities that damage them: the Johnsonian style is much less an unabridged-dictionary creature than used to be alleged: so preposterous a passage as this (from *The Rambler* Number 20)—". . . when from the adscititious happiness all the deductions are made by fear and casualty, there will remain nothing equiponderant to the security of truth. . . ."—is hard to find. The prevailing defect of the style is its gross and very personal exaggeration of the eighteenth-century notion that style, at the height of the civilized elegance which the Augustans felicitated themselves on having achieved, is merely the

more or less shapely vessel of thought. Since for Johnson the
public moralist all serious thought is a reminder of entropy and
the end of the world, he does everything he can to excogitate
and adorn, the more mechanically and tautologically the better, a manner of statement that will disguise the anarchic des-
peration of the matter:

> The general voice of mankind, civil and barbarous, con-
> fesses that the mind and body are at variance, and that neither
> can be made happy by its proper gratifications, but at the ex-
> pence of the other; that a pampered body will darken the mind,
> and an enlightened mind will macerate the body. And none have
> failed to confer their esteem on those who prefer intellect to
> sense, who controul their lower by their higher faculties, and
> forget the wants and desires of animal life for rational disquisi-
> tions or pious contemplations.

The very idea of desire can't be risked; it is so perilous that
Johnson surrounds it with tattered blankets of allegory and
mythological metaphor:

> Nothing is more fatal to happiness or virtue, than that con-
> fidence which flatters us with an opinion of our own strength,
> and by assuring us of the power of retreat precipitates us into
> hazard. Some may safely venture further than others into the
> regions of delight, lay themselves more open to the golden
> shafts of pleasure, and advance nearer to the residence of the
> Sirens; but he that is best armed with constancy and reason is
> yet vulnerable in one part or other, and to every man there is a
> point fixed, beyond which if he passes he will not easily return.
> It is certainly most wise, as it is most safe, to stop before he
> touches the utmost limit, since every step of advance will more
> and more entice him to go forward, till he shall at last enter the
> recesses of voluptuousness, and sloth and despondency close the
> passage behind him.

No epigram would have seemed more pernicious to Johnson than Blake's "The road of excess leads to the palace of wisdom." Johnson requires no advice to be excessive: he is all appetite, incapable of restraint except by absolute suppression.
"Every thing about his character and manners," says Boswell,
"was forcible and violent; there never was any moderation;

many a day did he fast, many a year did he refrain from wine; but when he did eat, it was voraciously; when he did drink wine, it was copiously. . . ."

> When at table, he was totally absorbed in the business of the moment; his looks seemed rivetted to his plate; nor would he, unless when in very high company, say one word, or even pay the least attention to what was said by others, till he had satisfied his appetite, which was so fierce, and indulged with such intenseness, that while in the act of eating, the veins of his forehead swelled, and generally a strong perspiration was visible. To those whose sensations were delicate, this could not but be disgusting; and it was doubtless not very suitable to the character of a philosopher, who should be distinguished by self-command. But it must be owned, that Johnson, though he could be rigidly *abstemious*, was not a *temperate* man, either in eating or drinking. He could refrain, but he could not use moderately. He told me, that he had fasted two days without inconvenience, and that he had never been hungry but once. They who beheld with wonder how much he eat upon all occasions when his dinner was to his taste, could not easily conceive what he must have meant by hunger . . .

Johnson is an unhappy ogre at the feast of life. His appetite appalls the other guests and soon enough himself; its inordinateness is the guarantee of its ultimate failure; excess as much as abstinence is a *memento mori:*

> . . . as we advance forward into the crowds of life, innumerable delights sollicit our inclinations, and innumerable cares distract our attention; the time of youth is passed in noisy frolicks; manhood is led on from hope to hope, and from project to project; the dissoluteness of pleasure, the inebriation of success, the ardour of expectation, and the vehemence of competition, chain down the mind alike to the present scene, nor is it remembered how soon this mist of trifles must be scattered, and the bubbles that float upon the rivulet of life be lost for ever in the gulph of eternity. . . .

At the edge of eternity, within a month of his death, seventy-five years old, the victim of a paralytic stroke, suffering from asthma and dropsy, constipated, tormented by insomnia, barely able to walk, even then he cannot be moderate or simply yield: for recreation he drives out in a friend's coach ("I struggle hard for life," he writes to Dr. Burney. "I take physick, and take air; my friend's chariot is always ready. We have run this morning twenty-four miles, and could run forty-eight more. *But who can run the race with death?*"); "such was his intellectual ardour even at this time," says Boswell, "that he said to one friend, 'Sir, I look upon every day to be lost, in which I do not make a new acquaintance'; and to another, when talking of his illness, 'I will be conquered; I will not capitulate' "; alone, he doses himself ferociously with a whole pharmacopoeia of emetics, cathartics, and narcotics, administers enemas to himself often several times daily, and in his "Sick Man's Journal" in Latin ("medical treatises should be in Latin") notes everything—dosages, food and drink, quantity of urine, quantity and quality of stool, amount of sleep, apparent changes in the state of his mind and body (together at last!).

"His figure was large and well formed," says Boswell, "and his countenance of the cast of an ancient statue; yet his appearance was rendered strange and somewhat uncouth, by convulsive cramps, by the scars of that distemper which it was once imagined the royal touch could cure, and by a slovenly mode of dress. He had the use only of one eye; yet so much does mind govern and even supply the deficiency of organs, that his visual perceptions, as far as they extended, were uncommonly quick and accurate. So morbid was his temperament, that he never knew the natural joy of a free and vigorous use of his limbs: when he walked, it was like the struggling gait of one in fetters; when he rode, he had no command or direction of his horse, but was carried as if in a balloon." Mrs. Thrale reports that he told her husband once "that he had never sought to please till past thirty years old, considering the matter as hopeless." "With all possible . . . delicacy" Boswell states that Johnson's "conduct, after he came to London, and had associated with Savage and others, was not so strictly virtuous, in one respect, as when he was a younger man. It was well known, that his amorous inclinations were uncommonly strong and impetuous." Boswell "never knew a man laugh

more heartily"; "I have known him at times exceedingly divert-
ed at what seemed to others a very small sport": he and Boswell learned that a friend of theirs had had a will drawn by a
lawyer they were visiting, and Johnson

> . . . laughed immoderately, without any reason that we could
> perceive, at our friend's making his will; called him the *testator*,
> and added, "I dare say, he thinks he has done a mighty thing.
> He won't stay till he gets home to his seat in the country, to
> produce this wonderful deed: he'll call up the landlord of the
> first inn on the road; and after a suitable preface upon mortality
> and the uncertainty of life, will tell him that he should not delay
> making his will; and here, Sir, will he say, is my will, which I
> have just made, with the assistance of one of the ablest lawyers
> in the kingdom; and he will read it to him (laughing all the
> time). He believes he has made this will; but he did not make it:
> you, Chambers, made it for him. I trust you have had more
> conscience than to make him say, 'being of sound understand-
> ing'; ha, ha, ha! I hope he has left me a legacy. I'd have his will
> turned into verse, like a ballad." . . .
>
> Mr. Chambers did not by any means relish this jocularity
> upon a matter of which *pars magna fuit*, and seemed impatient
> till he got rid of us. Johnson could not stop his merriment, but
> continued it all the way till we got without the Temple-gate. He
> then burst into such a fit of laughter, that he appeared to be al-
> most in a convulsion; and, in order to support himself, laid hold
> of one of the posts at the side of the foot pavement, and sent
> forth peals so loud, that in the silence of the night his voice
> seemed to resound from Temple-bar to Fleet-ditch.

He was immobilized and irrepressible. Boswell notes that
Johnson "feared death, but he feared nothing else, not even
what might occasion death. . . . One day, at Mr. Beauclerk's
house in the country, when two large dogs were fighting, he
went up to them, and beat them till they separated; and at
another time, when told of the danger there was that a gun
might burst if charged with many balls, he put in six or seven,
and fired it off against a wall. Mr. Langton told me, that when
they were swimming together near Oxford, he cautioned Dr.
Johnson against a pool, which was reckoned particularly dangerous; upon which Johnson directly swam into it. He told me

himself that one night he was attacked in the street by four men, to whom he would not yield, but kept them all at bay, till the watch came up, and carried both him and them to the roundhouse." Saying that Johnson "feared death, but . . . nothing else," Boswell momentarily forgets—what was well known among their circle of friends—that Johnson feared madness also: indeed there is evidence, in a letter by Johnson (in French!) to Mrs. Thrale and in some guarded remarks she confides to her diary, that her responsibility, when Johnson while residing in her home anticipated an onset, was to chain and manacle him in his locked room, enforce this "confinement and severity" (as she referred to it) with a whip, and keep the keys till he felt able to trust his faculties again. At every age he was a man of unaccommodatable passions: "How many Times," exclaims Mrs. Thrale in her diary, "has this great, this formidable Doctor Johnson kissed my hand, ay & my foot too upon his knees!" When he wrote his reluctant farewell letter to her—he was seventy-four—he wrote like the broken-hearted lover he was as he thanked her for "that kindness which soothed twenty years of a life radically wretched."

If he had been Dickens or Dostoevsky, he would have written disorderly melodramatic triple-decker novels brimming with incidents from the common life that was as much his element as theirs. Instead he wrote poets' biographies as austere as lighthouses, weighty eighteenth-century poems and superb eighteenth-century criticism, an epochal dictionary, a brilliantly annotated edition of Shakespeare (in which, without questioning Shakespeare's primacy, Johnson was the last and most astute English critic to suggest that the "licentiousness" of Shakespeare's diction didn't necessarily contribute to the unshackled expressiveness of the English language), moral essays and romances rather too categorical and funereal even for the taste of the time, and he spent his life in other people's drawing-rooms talking unstoppably into the night: " 'I lie down (said he) that my acquaintance may sleep; but I lie down to endure oppressive misery, and soon rise again to pass the night in anxiety and pain.' By this pathetic manner," comments Mrs. Thrale, "he used to shock me from quitting his company," which he made "exceedingly entertaining when he had once forced one, by his vehement lamentations and piercing reproofs, not to quit the room, but to sit quietly and make tea for him, as I often did in London till four o'clock in the morning."

The strangest fact of all about Johnson is that he is a character in other people's books. Our sense of his unprecedented magnitude depends on vivid and particular accounts by others, who—themselves figures bounded by their somewhat complacent century—could not have known how far his life was from being the exemplary eighteenth-century life they must have been convinced it would seem to an admiring posterity. If the vain and shrewd Mrs. Thrale hadn't pampered the famous old man and noted him down in the very pulsations of his nature—

> To recollect . . . and to repeat the sayings of Dr. Johnson, is almost all that can be done by the writers of his life; as his life, at least since my acquaintance with him, consisted in little else than talking, when he was not absolutely employed in some serious piece of work; and whatever work he did, seemed so much below his powers of performance, that he appeared the idlest of all human beings; ever musing till he was called out to converse, and conversing till the fatigue of his friends, or the promptitude of his own temper to take offence, consigned him back again to silent meditation.

—if (in a book immeasurably greater than the collected works of its subject) Boswell had not recorded him triumphantly talking away on every one of the world's questions in a thousand drawing-rooms, if all that remained of him was his writing, then we might make clever guesses at his personal virtues and shortcomings and even concede his idiosyncratic greatness but we would not begin to imagine how prodigious a phenomenon we had missed.

His marvelous powers of conversation are, in his formal writing, confined and often smothered by the self-mortifying compulsion to set down not personal casualty but, as his contemporaries and his conscience saw it, universal truth. In the tiny fragment, written in his sixties, of a memoir of his childhood, he tantalizes us with intimations of what he might have written if he hadn't been the lifelong prisoner of himself:

This Whitsuntide, I and my brother were sent to pass some time at Birmingham; I believe, a fortnight. Why such boys were sent to trouble other houses, I cannot tell. My mother had some opinion that much improvement was to be had by changing the mode of life. My uncle Harrison was a widower; and his house was kept by Sally Ford, a young woman of such sweetness of temper, that I used to say she had no fault. We lived most at uncle Ford's, being much caressed by my aunt, a good-natured coarse woman, easy of converse, but willing to find something to censure in the absent. My uncle Harrison did not much like us, nor did we like him. He was a very mean and vulgar man, drunk every night, but drunk with little drink, very peevish, very proud, very ostentatious, but, luckily, not rich. At my aunt Ford's I eat so much of a boiled leg of mutton, that she used to talk of it. My mother, who had lived in a narrow sphere, and was then affected by little things, told me seriously that it would hardly ever be forgotten. Her mind, I think, was afterwards much enlarged, or greater evils wore out the care of less. . . .

In making, I think, the first exercise under Holbrook [his schoolmaster], I perceived the power of continuity of attention, of application not suffered to wander or to pause. I was writing at the kitchen windows, as I thought, alone, and turning my head saw Sally dancing. I went on without notice, and had finished almost without perceiving that any time had elapsed. This close attention I have seldom in my whole life attained.

"A story is a specimen of human manners," he said to Mrs. Thrale, "and derives its sole value from its truth." The glow of his memoir is in its relying solely on the truth, with which in this instance art or calculation seems to have nothing to do.

Truth is the first test of everything: "Johnson was known to be so rigidly attentive to it," says Boswell, "that even in his common conversation the slightest circumstance was mentioned with exact precision. The knowledge of his having such a principle and habit made his friends have a perfect reliance on the truth of every thing that he told, however it might have been doubted if told by many others. As an instance of this, I may mention an odd incident which he related as having happened to him one night in Fleet-street. 'A gentlewoman (said he) begged I would give her my arm to assist her in crossing the street, which I accordingly did; upon which she offered me a shilling, supposing me to be the watchman. I perceived that she was somewhat in liquor.' This, if told by most people, would have been thought an invention; when told by Johnson it was believed by his friends as much as if they had seen what passed."

The important truth is the truth of human manners: to a friend commenting on the beauty of the landscape through which they were traveling, Johnson retorted that "a blade of grass is always a blade of grass,[2] whether in one country or another: let us if we *do* talk, talk about something; men and women are my subjects of enquiry; let us see how these differ from those we have left behind." According to Mrs. Thrale,

> . . . no kind of conversation pleased him less I think, than when the subject was historical fact or general polity. "What shall we learn from *that* stuff (said he)? let us not fancy like Swift that we are exalting a woman's character by telling how she
>
> > Could name the ancient heroes round,
> > Explain for what they were renown'd, &c."

I must not however lead my readers to suppose that he meant to reserve such talk for *men's* company as a proof of pre-eminence. "He never (as he expressed it) desired to hear of the *Punic war* while he lived: such conversation was lost time (he said), and carried one away from common life, leaving no ideas behind which would serve *living wight* as warning or direction." . . .

I asked him once concerning the conversation powers of a gentleman with whom I was myself unacquainted—"He talked to me at club one day (replies our Doctor) concerning Catiline's conspiracy—so I withdrew my attention, and thought about Tom Thumb."

---

[2]Johnson's one functioning eye was very myopic, and not in any case qualified to do much distinguishing between one blade of grass and another. During a visit to a country estate, Johnson was "taken out to walk in the garden. The master of the house, thinking it proper to introduce something scientifick into the conversation, addressed him thus: 'Are you a botanist, Dr. Johnson?' 'No, Sir, (answered Johnson,) I am not a botanist; and, (alluding, no doubt, to his near sightedness) should I wish to become a botanist, I must first turn myself into a reptile.' "

Modern politics fared no better. . . . In the year 1777, or thereabouts, when all the talk was of an invasion, he said most pathetically one afternoon, "Alas! alas! how this unmeaning stuff spoils all my comfort in my friends' conversation! Will the people never have done with it; and shall I never hear a sentence again without the *French* in it? Here is no invasion coming, and you *know* there is none. Let the vexatious and frivolous talk alone, or suffer it at least to teach you *one* truth; and learn by this perpetual echo of even unapprehended distress, how historians magnify events expected, or calamities endured; when you know they are at this very moment collecting all the big words they can find, in which to describe a consternation never felt, for a misfortune which never happened. Among all your lamentations, who eats the less? Who sleeps the worse, for one general's ill success, or another's capitulation? *Oh, pray* let us hear no more of it!'"

He was a great, good, kind, loving, companionable man. Once when Miss Helen Maria Williams, "an elegant and accomplished young lady," was in his company, "he asked her to sit down by him, which she did, and upon her inquiring how he was, he answered, 'I am very ill indeed, Madam. I am very ill even when you are near me; what should I be were you at a distance?' " Boswell

. . . was surprised at his talking without reserve in the publick postcoach of the state of his affairs; "I have (said he,) about the world I think above a thousand pounds, which I intend shall afford Frank [his servant] an annuity of seventy pounds a year." Indeed his openness with people at a first interview was remarkable. He said once to Mr. Langton, "I think I am like Squire Richard in *The Journey to London, 'I'm never strange in a strange place.' "* He was truly *social.* He strongly censured what is much too common in England among persons of condition,— maintaining an absolute silence, when unknown to each other; as for instance, when occasionally brought together in a room before the master or mistress of the house has appeared. "Sir, that is being so uncivilised as not to understand the common rights of humanity."

He loved and needed his hosts of friends more continuously and more intensely than any of them could love and need

him in return; he loved women often for themselves and always
as the special consolation of men; he loved children[3] and the
young ("you have at least a chance for virtue till age has with-
ered its very root"); he had himself been miserably poor for
many years, and

> . . . loved the poor [observes Mrs. Thrale] as I never yet saw
> any one else do, with an earnest desire to make them happy.—
> What signifies, says some one, giving halfpence to common beg-
> gars? they only lay it out in gin or tobacco. "And why should
> they be denied such sweeteners of their existence (says John-
> son)? it is surely very savage to refuse them every possible ave-
> nue to pleasure, reckoned too coarse for our own acceptance.
> Life is a pill which none of us can bear to swallow without gild-
> ing; yet for the poor we delight in stripping it still barer, and are
> not ashamed to shew even visible displeasure, if ever the bitter
> taste is taken from their mouths." In consequence of these prin-
> ciples he nursed whole nests of people in his house, where the
> lame, the blind, the sick, and the sorrowful found a sure retreat
> from all the evils whence his little income could secure
> them . . .

The strongest essays by this Christian Tory, who thunder-
ously supported rank and subordination, are devoted to attacking capital punishment, parental tyranny, vivisection, war and
other conflicts about property, debtors' prisons; advocating the
abolition of imprisonment for debt, he doesn't hesitate to hold
the creditor more culpable (because impelled by meaner vices)
than the debtor:

> It is vain to continue an institution, which experience shews
> to be ineffectual. We have now imprisoned one generation of

---

[3]"The remembrance of what had passed in his own childhood made Mr.
Johnson very solicitous to preserve the felicity of children; and when he had
persuaded Dr. Sumner to remit the tasks usually given to fill up boys' time
during the holidays, he rejoiced exceedingly in the success of his negociation,
and told . . . [Mrs. Thrale] that he had never ceased representing to all the
eminent schoolmasters in England, the absurd tyranny of poisoning the hour
of permitted pleasure, by keeping future misery before the children's eyes,
and tempting them by bribery or falsehood to evade it. 'Bob Sumner (said
he), however, I have at length prevailed upon: I know not indeed whether his
tenderness was persuaded, or his reason convinced, but the effect will always
be the same.' . . ."

debtors after another, but we do not find that their numbers lessen. We have now learned, that rashness and imprudence will not be deterred from taking credit; let us try whether fraud and avarice may be more easily restrained from giving it.

Swift's *saeva indignatio* is more noticed, but Johnson's indignation has none of the misanthropy and self-congratulation of Swift's. Johnson's has always an unencumbered straightforwardness of motive, as when in the greatest book review ever written he assesses the silliness of the "philosopher" Soame Jenyns, who in his *Free Enquiry into the Nature and Origin of Evil* derived a system of benignant universal hierarchy from Pope's *Essay on Man* ("Whatever is, is right"):

> That hope and fear are inseparably or very frequently connected with poverty, and riches, my surveys of life have not informed me. The milder degrees of poverty are sometimes supported by hope, but the more severe often sink down in motionless despondence. Life must be seen before it can be known. This author and *Pope* perhaps never saw the miseries which they imagine thus easy to be born. The poor indeed are insensible of many little vexations which sometimes imbitter the possessions and pollute the enjoyment, of the rich. They are not pained by casual incivility, or mortified by the mutilation of a compliment; but this happiness is like that of a malefactor who ceases to feel the cords that bind him when the pincers are tearing his flesh.

Nor will this champion of subordination accept Jenyns' view that education is not for the poor:

> Though it should be granted that those who are *born to poverty and drudgery* should not be *deprived* by an *improper education* of the *opiate* of *ignorance*; even this concession will not be of much use to direct our practice, unless it be determined who are those that are *born to poverty*. To entail irreversible poverty upon generation after generation only because the ancestor happened to be poor, is in itself cruel, if not unjust, and is wholly contrary to the maxims of a commercial nation, which always suppose and promote a rotation of property, and offer every individual a chance of mending his condition by his diligence. Those who communicate literature to the son of a poor man, consider him as one not born to poverty, but to the

necessity of deriving a better fortune from himself. In this attempt, as in others, many fail and many succeed. Those that fail will feel their misery more acutely; but since poverty is now confessed to be such a calamity as cannot be born without the opiate of insensibility, I hope the happiness of those whom education enables to escape from it, may turn the ballance against that exacerbation which the others suffer.

I am always afraid of determining on the side of envy or cruelty.

And Johnson's indignation clarifies the shape and mass of his style into pure kinetic energy when, sardonically examining Jenyns' supposition that human suffering is justifiable because it is the will of superior beings to whom we are as animals are to us, he concludes with a fantasia on the theme of human fatuity:

> As we drown whelps and kittens, they amuse themselves now and then with sinking a ship, and stand round the fields of *Blenheim*, or the walls of *Prague*, as we encircle a cock-pit. As we shoot a bird flying, they take a man in the midst of his business or pleasure, and knock him down with an apoplexy. Some of them, perhaps, are virtuosi, and delight in the operations of an asthma, as a human philosopher in the effects of the air pump. To swell a man with a tympany is as good sport as to blow a frog. Many a merry bout have these frolic beings at the vicissitudes of an ague, and good sport it is to see a man tumble with an epilepsy, and revive and tumble again, and all this he knows not why. . . .
>
> One sport the merry malice of these beings has found means of enjoying to which we have nothing equal or similar. They now and then catch a mortal proud of his parts, and flattered either by the submission of those who court his kindness, or the notice of those who suffer him to court theirs. A head thus prepared for the reception of false opinions, and the projection of vain designs, they easily fill with idle notions, till in time they make their plaything an author . . .

The ogre who ate up Jenyns skin, bones, and all was not —though Jenyns must have thought he was[4]—one of those su-

---

[4]Jenyns waited thirty years—till after Johnson's death!—for his revenge. "Some time after Dr. Johnson's death," says Boswell in a footnote, "there

perior beings who prescribe and savor human suffering. He was
not even a mortal proud of his parts. His powers, though they
repelled evil and affectation and illuminated the world for everyone who knew him, could not exorcise his fear of the ven-
geance of God:

> I have now begun the sixtieth year of my life. How the last
> year has past I am unwilling to terrify myself with thinking.
> This day has been past in great perturbation. I was distracted at
> Church in an uncommon degree, and my distress has had very
> little intermission. . . .

Twelve years later, another birthday prayer commemorated "a
life radically wretched":

> I have forgotten or neglected my resolutions or purposes
> [which] I now humbly and timorously renew. Surely I shall not
> spend my whole life with my own total disapprobation. Perhaps
> God may grant me now to begin a wiser and a better life.
>   Almighty God, my Creator and Preserver, who hast per-
> mitted me to begin another year, look with mercy upon my
> wretchedness and frailty. Rectify my thoughts, relieve my per-
> plexities, strengthen my purposes, and reform my doings. Let
> encrease of years bring encrease of Faith, Hope, and Chari-
> ty. . . .

It would never have occurred to him that he had in fact
done enough, he could not help remembering how much had
been promised and how much left undone in the terrifying
range of his powers.

---

appeared in the newspapers and magazines an illiberal and petulant attack
upon him, in the form of an Epitaph, under the name of Mr. Soame Jenyns,
very unworthy of that gentleman, who had quietly submitted to the critical
lash while Johnson lived. It assumed, as characteristicks of him, all the vulgar circumstances of abuse which had circulated amongst the ignorant. It was
an unbecoming indulgence of puny resentment, at a time when he himself was
at a very advanced age, and had a near prospect of descending to the grave."

V.
Trollope

Trollope had no business writing so many books, which moreover had no business being so very good. Even James Pope Hennessy, in his generally informative and sometimes ungrudging critical biography,[1] can't refrain from fits of temper calculated to prove that nobody's perfect, no not Trollope for all his skill, intelligence, wit, humor, energy, vivacity, reliability, thoroughness, and disgustingly exemplary professional habits. Trollope tells us, in his autobiography, that he got himself awakened every morning in time to carry through before breakfast his daily three-hour stint of authorship; and here, a century later, gets his knuckles rapped for *idleness*:

> He has accused Thackeray of idleness—presumably because he did not begin writing at five thirty of a winter's morning—and of allowing his characters to proliferate in an uncontrolled manner; "his pen was not firm." It never occurred to Anthony that he was, as a matter of fact, a very great deal idler than Thackeray had ever been—for Thackeray would agree to shorten stories or articles at his editor's request, whereas Trollope, on being asked by Longman's to reduce *Barchester Towers* by one-third had flown into a rage and refused. . . . One cannot but presume that his literary output would have distinctly benefited

[1] *Anthony Trollope* (Boston, 1971).

had he spent several mornings a month asleep in bed until a human hour for rising. But he himself was perfectly satisfied that his morning's ration of novel-writing, timed to the second by the gold repeater on his desk, was a sign of an industrious virtue to which more frivolous or spasmodic writers lacked the courage to aspire. Scribbling two thousand words before breakfast, never rereading them, scarcely correcting the text save in proof-sheets for printers' errors—does not all this essentially smack of a gross and careless form of self-indulgence? Had he disciplined his pen with the same harsh rigour as that with which he disciplined his body to blunder from bed to desk at dawn in response to poor old Barney MacIntyre's early-bird call with a cup of coffee, he could undoubtedly have achieved a concision which he too seldom displays. . . .

But, as Pope Hennessy could have reminded himself by glancing at Chapter XV of the *Autobiography,* "Anthony" didn't begin writing at five-thirty and did in fact reread: between five-thirty a.m. and six he went over what he had written the day before; and "that . . . [a completed manuscript] should be read twice at least before it goes to the printers, I take to be a matter of course." Also, the output was two thousand five hundred words per morning, not two thousand. Nor would Pope Hennessy, in a less fretful mood, have been likely to imply, as he does here, that (1) *Barchester Towers* would be better for being a third shorter, and (2) the novelist who produced a larger quantity of first-rate novels than any other novelist on record would "undoubtedly" have written still better novels if he had had worse habits (and if he had given up his active job at the post office, and his uneventful but time-consuming happy marriage, and his beloved fox-hunting, and his founding and editing of magazines, and running for Parliament, and his London clubs at which he was a boisterous talker and a busy official, and his voyages to Ireland, the Continent, the West Indies, the United States, Egypt, Australia, Ceylon, South Africa). If only Trollope had taken writing seriously, if he had sweated and fumed and stared at blank walls for weeks on end before extruding three sentences that burn with a hard gemlike flame! Instead, at home or in a ship or railway carriage or wherever he happened to be traveling or visiting, he scribbled away at a thousand words an hour (he counted every word, two hundred and fifty per page) from six a.m. to eight-thirty and could then, as he once did, come down to breakfast remarking, "I have just been making my twenty-seventh proposal of marriage." How was it possible for him to turn out (besides travel books, collections of short stories, letters, miles of post-office reports and proposals, as well as by his own account "political articles, critical, social and sporting articles, for periodicals without number")—how did such a monster of sloth manage to turn out forty-seven novels, most of them Victorian double- and triple-deckers, almost all of them absorbing and worthy of thoughtful attention, many excellent, a dozen or more among the glories of English fiction?

Pope Hennessy has other complaints. According to him, "Trollope was perhaps abnormally conscious of the value, the duties and the status of the English gentleman": for instance, on his children's baptismal certificates Trollope "described himself not as a postal surveyor but as a 'Gentleman' " (though Pope Hennessy doesn't mention the interesting precedent of Shakespeare, who, having obtained a coat-of-arms for his father, described himself in late documents not as an actor and stagehand but as a "Gentleman"). Or Trollope lacks a social conscience:

> . . . the smoky caverns of human misery and despair into which both the landlords and the ironmasters of the Midlands and the North were herding a people until recently pastoral seem not to have impinged on Anthony's consciousness at all. His only references to the industrial scene in Britain were to use these as explaining why some of his characters were so enviably rich. In the opening pages of *Mr Scarborough's Family*, for example, a new industrial potteries development is mentioned simply as explaining why the annual income of the pagan old squire of Tretton Park had increased from £4000 a year to £20,000.
> . . . Charles Dickens, for whom Anthony affected contempt, would have taken us by the hand and led us in amongst the white-faced, cursing factory girls and the stunted children working at the furnaces of the Tretton delf factory. Emile Zola and Maxence van der Meersch would have spared us no grim detail. But then none of these novelists were bound by a self-imposed

limitation to write for well-brought-up English girls and for them alone. . . .

But Trollope treated, quite uncompromisingly, problems of private feeling and personal responsibility that may have been more troubling to well-brought-up English girls than Dickens's social indignation. Pope Hennessy's sneer at Trollope's "self-imposed limitation" is unpersuasive: Dickens was not so bold, nor Trollope so timid, as the rhetoric insists: Dickens's sales and the evening readings aloud of his newest novel at every Victorian hearth don't seem to have been curtailed by his social conscience, which may now and then have sounded to some of his less excitable contemporaries like campaign oratory. Trollope was a meliorist who, believing that social change is necessary, held that the British parliamentary system is its proper instrument or at any rate authorizes it after the fact: the belief may be wrong or obsolete, but it isn't contemptible. (Much of the solidity of the very fine series of Palliser novels is in the episodes of parliamentary maneuver and debate.) Nobody was less interested than Trollope in the sociological axiom that a man or woman is unfairly incapacitated by disadvantages of class and upbringing, and nobody more interested in the data of social conditions: in his travel books, Trollope described "how a society was organized—politically, economically, and culturally. It is said that when Henry Adams visited Ceylon he sat for half an hour under the shoots of Buddha's bo-tree. Trollope had probably never heard of Buddha's bo-tree, but he leaves little to be said about the history of the coffee industry."[2] Trollope believed that a society is the sum of what the people in it do, he hated inertia and entropy, he wanted to know how things worked and he liked them in working order.

He was very sparing of pathos. Pope Hennessy complains of the dryness and reserve of the *Autobiography*: pages of

---

[2]Bradford A. Booth, *Anthony Trollope* (Bloomington, 1958), p. 80. Trollope had probably even heard of Buddha's bo-tree. By his fifty-eighth year he had a personal library of five thousand volumes, and he was a devoted reader: "That I can read and be happy while I am reading, is a great blessing. Could I remember, as some men do, what I read, I should have been able to call myself an educated man."

bookkeeping about the money earned by each of Trollope's books, "maddeningly reticent" allusions to his marriage ("My marriage was like the marriage of other people and of no special interest to any one except my wife and me"); yet how anybody can fail to be moved by Trollope's dry and reserved account of the terrible wretchedness of his boyhood and youth, or fail to be exhilarated by the bare assertion of miraculous and permanent change in his life as soon as he took the apparently hopeless job in Ireland, is a mystery that will have to be resolved by exasperated biographers.

Then Pope Hennessy, in alliance with Henry James, attacks certain Trollopian practices that he declines to consider innocuous:

> [*Is He Popenjoy?*] . . . has always, in my opinion, been underrated—owing, perhaps, to its almost criminally idiotic title. We have noticed before Trollope's deliberate selection, from time to time, of what Henry James deplored as "fantastic names." It has in the past been suggested that such fatal choices came from an attempt on Trollope's part to emulate Thackeray, although it seems to me far more likely that he was influenced by the Tudor and Jacobean playwrights, the reading of whose works had for some years provided his chief form of mental recreation. Even as late as Sheridan writers for the English stage often used a surname to indicate trade or psychology—we have only to think of Lady Sneerwell in *The School for Scandal.* Trollope, however, dealt out some of his titles and his surnames with a hand of lead: Lord Grassangrains "that well-known breeder of bullocks," or Lord Gossling of Gossling castle, whose family name is de Geese and whose eldest son bears the courtesy title of Lord Giblet. . . .

It's hard to be patient with a critic who can't rejoice at such an inspiration as "Lord Giblet" (and distinguish it from the mere function denoted by such a mechanical doubling as "Lady Sneerwell"). Trollope's favorite and most impressive character succeeds to the title Duke of Omnium, his ducal house is Gatherum Castle: these are names which, like other names, take getting used to before they signify the person who bears them. And why not rejoice at the prodigality of an author who writes too many substantial novels to be bothered finding suitably stuffy names for all of them? Sometimes *Is He Popenjoy?* or *Can You Forgive Her?* or *He Knew He Was Right* will have to do. Pope Hennessy won't even accept Trollope's occasional brief Chaucerian appearances in the story ("I quite feel that an apology is due for beginning a novel with two long, dull chapters full of description"), and cites James on Trollope's " '. . . suicidal satisfaction in reminding the reader that the story he was telling was only, after all, a make-believe. . . . These little slaps at credulity are very discouraging. . . .' "; as if the novelist were a stage magician whose effects depend on the public's being kept in the dark about all those explicable tricks.

There's just too much of Trollope, it's all bang in the open with no tricks, and if we don't watch out he'll be getting on our precious nerves. A nearly excusable provocation is the fifth novel of the Palliser series, *The Prime Minister.* This may be the weakest of the series: the principal male character in one of the two main plots appears from the outset as an unreformable scoundrel of a simple money-grubbing sort; his victim is one of Trollope's notorious obstinate moonstruck females who get into their heads the notion that a first infatuation is everlasting love and won't renounce it for family, friends, other suitors, plus twenty-two proofs that the man is a scoundrel; and the plot they share is a glacially slow progress of the obvious (though, as usual in Trollope, each incident taken by itself is reasonable and engaging). But there's more. The other main plot of the novel considers the Duke of Omnium as Prime Minister. This plot, too, advances with glacial slowness as it presents—over the long span of time and with the density and minute variations of detail that such a large, deliberate action requires—the history of a parliamentary government: the question is what, after all, could be duller in a novel than to examine the favoring circumstances, the crisis, the grasping of the opportunity, the triumph and consolidation, the signs of instability as personal ambitions begin to diverge, the miscalculations and bad luck, the defects of temperament, the gradual and unimpedable erosion, and at length the long foreseen and long delayed collapse? yet here the slowness is right, inevitable, careful, affecting, and particularly appropriate to the complicated, self-tortured, inarticulate nature of the Duke himself. It needs to be added that even Plot No. 1, mostly a bore, comes to an astonishing climax: the great scene, reported as from an astronomical distance by an all-seeing observer, in which the scoundrel, plainly not quite resolute till the final moment, throws himself at last from a railway station platform into the path of a train.[3]

---

[3]"It has recently been discovered," says Pope Hennessy (p. 331), though he doesn't say by whom or how or when or where, "that Tolstoy read *The Prime Minister* whilst he was writing *Anna Karenina*. He called it 'a beautiful book.' Lopez's suicide under a railway train at Tenby Junction may indeed have sealed Anna Karenina's fate, suggesting to Tolstoy a new and horrifying form of sudden death." But it is certain that Anna's fate was already sealed, though the triple coincidence (the virtually identical suicides, the virtual simultaneity of the books, Tolstoy's happening on the other while writing his own) is startling to say the least. *The Prime Minister*, finished in 1874, was published in installments between November 1875 and June 1876; published complete, in two volumes, in May 1876. *Anna Karenina* was first published in installments beginning January 1875; Tolstoy finished the novel on April 15, 1877. It is therefore certain that Trollope could not have seen *Anna Karenina* before completing *The Prime Minister*. (There is indeed no evidence that he ever heard of Tolstoy.) It is equally certain that Tolstoy could not have read *The Prime Minister* before he had clearly prefigured, in sections of *Anna Karenina* already published, the circumstances of Anna's death: Chapter XVIII of Part I (published in February 1875) already foreshadows Anna's death—a man commits suicide by throwing himself under the train from which, arriving at the railway station in Moscow, Anna makes her entrance (she herself says, "It's a bad omen") into the novel. Moreover, at least four years before there is any likelihood at all of Tolstoy's having got hold of a copy of *The Prime Minister*, Tolstoy had interested himself in an event that his biographers and critics have always considered the event that "sealed Anna Karenina's fate": "The description of Anna's dead body in the shed of the station yard in Chapter 6 of the last part is autobiographical in the sense that, according to a note in . . . [Countess Tolstoy's] diary, Tolstoy himself had witnessed such a scene. The woman, who was called Anna, was a discarded mistress of one of Tolstoy's neighbors and she committed suicide by throwing herself under a train. Tolstoy, Sonia records, saw her after the post-mortem in the railway shed naked and with her skull and body cut open" (David Magarshack, Foreword to his translation of *Anna Karenina*, Signet, 1961, p. xv). The suicide occurred on January 4, 1872; Tolstoy saw the body the following day. Without divine assistance or conscientious scholarship, we may never know what led Pope Hennessy to draw such an inference (and add his own few knots to the tangled skein of literary history), since he doesn't let us check his source, and seems unaware of the public information about *Anna Karenina* against which his inference ought to be have been checked.

Pope Hennessy finds *The Prime Minister* altogether a bore; and perhaps the best that can be said of his chronic biliousness is that he's not a Trollopian, beaming imperviously on all the many sacred volumes as he constructs maps and genealogies of the master's imaginary provinces. Much of the book is given over to discussions of most of Trollope's work: the discussions tend to be rather brusque, but—except when they founder on some such spiky aesthetic reef as Trollope's working habits—sensible and judicious without necessarily persuading us that *The Vicar of Bullhampton* also is altogether a bore or that *The Small House at Allington*, characteristic and unremarkable Trollope, is the "supreme work of his art" or the stagy and solemn Madame Max Goesler in any way comparable to the perverse, fearless, sentimental, witty, unladylike, heartbroken, matchmaking, troublemaking, loyal, superb, and incomparable Lady Glencora ("the most winning and entertaining of any of Trollope's women—with the possible exception of Madame Max Goesler").

Pope Hennessy is effective and sympathetic on Trollope's early life and on his family, especially his redoubtable mother, the celebrated Fanny Trollope, author of *Domestic Manners of the Americans*. Mrs. Trollope began writing at the age of fifty as the family's sole provider and, nursing her brood of consumptives most of whom died over a period of a few years, kept writing on a schedule as regular as her son's till she had published one hundred and fifteen volumes (Trollope notes in the *Autobiography* that she, his historian brother Tom, and Trollope himself wrote "more books than were probably ever before produced by a single family"). What, however, makes Pope Hennessy's book a (somewhat qualified and crotchety) success is his talent—the biographer's indispensable talent—for choosing the right quotations; this one, for example, from *The Kellys and the O'Kellys*, Trollope's second novel (written in 1847), in which the young hero enjoys a typical meal aboard the canal-boat from Dublin:

> He made great play at the eternal half-boiled leg of mutton, floating in a bloody sea of grease, which always comes on the table three hours after the departure from Porto Bello. He, and

others equally gifted . . . swallowed huge collops of the raw animal and vast heaps of yellow turnips, till the pity with which a stranger would at first be inclined to contemplate the consumer of such unsavoury food, is transferred to the victim who has to provide the meal at two shillings a head. . . .

Or this one, from *Mr Scarborough's Family*, Trollope's forty-fifth novel (written in 1881), in which, recording some carefree talk between the honeymooners as they wander among the Alpine flowers, Trollope demonstrates that, even within the Victorian decorum, a great novelist is excluded from none of the secrets of intimacy, not indeed from the marriage-bed itself:

"Well, old girl!" he said, "and now what do you think of it all?"

"I'm not so very much older than I was when you took me, pet."

"Oh yes, you are. Half of your life has gone; you have settled down into the cares and duties of married life, none of which had been so much as thought of when you took me."

The husband is wearing "highlows" (hobnail boots), and he remarks that if he had worn them during his courtship she would have considered him "such an awkward fellow"—

"But now you must take my highlows as part of your duty."

"And you?"

"When a man loves a woman he falls in love with everything belonging to her. You don't wear highlows. Everything you possess as specially your own has to administer to my sense of love and beauty."

"I wish, I wish it might be so."

"There is no danger about that at all. But I have come before you on such an occasion as this as a kind of navvy. . . . And then there is ever so much more," he continued, "I don't think I snore."

"Indeed no! There isn't a sound comes from you. I sometimes look to see if I think you are alive."

Or this one, from *Miss Mackenzie* (written in 1864), invading the spinster's boudoir:

She got up and looked at herself in the mirror. She moved up her hair from off her ears, knowing where she would find a few that were grey, and shaking her head, as though owning to herself that she was old; but as her fingers ran almost involuntarily across her locks, her touch told her that they were soft and silken; she looked into her own eyes and saw that they were bright; and her hand touched the outline of her cheek, and she knew that something of the fresh bloom of youth was still there; and her lips parted, and there were her white teeth. . . . She pulled her scarf tighter across her own bosom, feeling her own form and then she leaned forward and kissed herself in the glass.

Here is Trollope himself, at the age of forty-six, defending himself against a friend's charge that he rates the joys of courtship above the joys of marriage:

As to myself personally, I have daily to wonder at the continued run of domestic & worldly happiness which has been granted me;—to wonder at it as well as to be thankful for it. I do so, fearing that my day also of misery must come; for we are told by so many teachers of all doctrines that pain of some sort is man's lot. But no pain or misery has as yet come to me since the day I married; & if any man should speak well of the married state, I should do so.

But I deny that I have done other. There is a sweet young blushing joy about the first acknowledged reciprocal love, which is like the bouquet of the first glass of wine from the bottle—It goes when it has been tasted. But for all that who will confuse the momentary aroma with the lasting joys of the still flowing bowl. May the Bowl still flow for both of us, and leave no touch of headache.

At the age of fifty-eight Trollope, suffering the promised day of misery, discloses to a friend that he has gone deaf in one ear:

I fancy I am going to be run over, and everybody seems to talk to me on the wrong side. I am told that a bone has grown up inside the orifice. Oh dear! One does not understand at all. Why should any bones grow, except useful, working bones? Why should anything go wrong in our bodies? Why should not we be all beautiful? Why should there be dread?—why death?—and, oh why, damnation?

And at sixty-seven, in the last year of his life, he denies that men grow old:

> I observe when people of my age are spoken of, they are described as effete and moribund, just burning down the last half-inch of the candle in the socket. I feel as though I should still like to make a "flare-up" with my half-inch. In spirit I could trundle a hoop about the streets, and could fall in love with a young woman as readily as ever; as she doesn't want me, I don't —but I could!

(For the past twenty years there had been just such an unattainable young woman in his life, the beautiful American Kate Field, whom in the language of love he acknowledges, without naming her, on one of the last pages of the *Autobiography*. They could be, and were, friends; and she and his wife were friends too.)

One quality of the man not plausibly deducible from his writing was his noisy and unsettling physical presence. At the dinner party where he met for the first time Thackeray, G. H. Lewes, and the painter John Millias, Trollope spent a blustery evening "contradicting everybody, then trying to mend the damage he had done by friendly words," as well as (according to the journalist George Augustus Sala) " 'going to sleep on sofas, chairs, or leaning against sideboards, and even somnolent while standing erect on the hearthrug.' " (Such catnapping, whatever its social consequences, no doubt made it easier for him to rise briskly at five every morning ready for hard labor.) "Sala had never before met anyone 'who could take so many spells of "forty winks" at unexpected moments, and then turn up quite wakeful, alert, and pugnacious. . . .' " On his second visit to the United States, in 1868 (he was on official post-office business), he attended a dinner together with James Russell Lowell, Oliver Wendell Holmes, and Ralph Waldo Emerson. Lowell's account of it is "our best, indeed our only, account of what an attempt to converse with Anthony Trollope was like":

> Dined the other day with Anthony Trollope; a big, red-faced, rather underbred Englishman of the bald-with-spectacles type.

A good roaring positive fellow who deafened me (sitting on his
right) till I thought of Dante's Cerberus. He says he goes to
work on a novel "just like a shoemaker on a shoe, only taking
care to make honest stitches." Gets up at five every day, does
all his writing before breakfast, and always writes just so many
pages a day. He and Dr Holmes were very entertaining. The
Autocrat started one or two hobbies, and charged, paradox in
rest—but it was pelting a rhinoceros with seed-pearl.

DR.　You don't know what Madeira is in England?

T.　I'm not so sure it's worth knowing.

DR.　Connoisseurship with us is a fine art. There are men who
　　will tell a dozen kinds, as Dr Waagen would know a Carlo
　　Dolci from a Guido.

T.　They might be better employed!

DR.　Whatever is worth doing is worth doing well.

T.　Ay, but that's begging the whole question. I don't admit
　　it's *worse* doing at all. If they earn their bread by it, it
　　may be *worse* doing (roaring).

DR.　But you may be assured—

T.　No, but I mayn't be asshorred. I don't intend to be as-
　　shorred (roaring louder)!

And so they went it. It was very funny. Trollope wouldn't give
him any chance. Meanwhile, Emerson and I, who sat between
them, crouched down out of range, and had some very good
talk, with the shot hurtling overhead. . . . I rather liked Trollope.

Pope Hennessy pays tribute, often, to Trollope's powers of
precise observation. "An intelligent Dublin lady, who knew
Anthony Trollope well in these earliest Irish days, used remini-
scently to say that 'his close looking into the commonest objects of daily life always reminded her of a woman in a shop
examining the materials for a new dress' "; and Trollope precisely vindicates the image as, writing about the United States
thirty years after his mother's book, he describes the wealthy
and fashionable New York woman dragging the long train of
her expensive dress behind her over the unspeakable pavement
"where the dogs have been, and chewers of tobacco, and everything concerned with filth except a scavenger." Ten years later,
passing through Salt Lake City, he decided to call on Brigham
Young (and records the encounter in a passage of the *Autobiography* that, unaccountably, Pope Hennessy doesn't use):

He received me in his doorway, not asking me to enter, and inquired whether I were not a miner. When I told him that I was not a miner, he asked me whether I earned my bread. I told him I did. "I guess you're a miner," said he. I again assured him that I was not. "Then how do you earn your bread?" I told him that I did so by writing books. "I'm sure you're a miner," said he. Then he turned upon his heel, went back into the house, and closed the door. I was properly punished, as I was vain enough to conceive that he would have heard my name.

Evidently Trollope's market didn't extend as far as Salt Lake City, and he never expected it to extend beyond his own century.

He wrote so much that he was afraid of flooding the market, and made a point of staying ahead of himself with several completed manuscripts locked away in his desk. He wrote till he died, and at his death there was enough on hand in the desk to supply the unsaturated market with a year or two of Trollope titles. Trollope would have been pleased.

VI.
Leavis on Dickens

If this[1] were a better book, its publication—so late in Leavis's very long career—might be an occasion for nervously congratulating the intractable old samurai on his services to literacy, not the least of which was to put the fear of retribution and ruin into the hearts of literary scholars and English Departments everywhere. Leavis has been whacking off heads for forty years now, as René Wellek once found out to his detriment, and the lecture-survey notion of literary history will never again be quite so voluminously smug. Leavis is a loner, a spoiler, an unclubbable man: even in the Scrutiny years he was megalithically *primus inter pares*, the sayer of the last stone word not only on the topics he chose for himself but on those introduced by his associates, as in a characteristic "rejoinder" to an essay by L. C. Knights—"I find myself with some embarrassment driven to point out . . ." (Leavis's politest way of intimating that his adversary is a criminal idiot). Doubtless his temper wasn't improved by Oxbridge's determination to suppress the upstart who presumed—from within the gates!— to dispute its taste and judgment, but then a kinder reception would have been unlikely to cheer him up either. Bernard

---

[1] F. R. and Q. D. Leavis, *Dickens the Novelist* (New York, 1970).

Shaw's criterion (which Shaw himself never took seriously), that the critic must be a pariah, that "his hand should be against every man's, and every man's hand against his," seems to have been invented for the purpose of predicting and vindicating Leavis. Braced by rage all these years against battalions of British dons and American professors, Leavis is in no mood, as the dedication of this book makes plain, to share anything with anybody except his wife:

> We dedicate this book to each other as proof, along with *Scrutiny* (of which for twenty-one years we sustained the main burden and the responsibility), of forty years and more of daily collaboration in living, university teaching, discussion of literature and the social and cultural context from which literature is born, and above all, devotion to the fostering of that true respect for creative writing, creative minds and, English literature being in question, the English tradition, without which literary criticism can have no validity and no life.

Perfection is or at least has to be its own reward. Its disadvantage is that it doesn't encourage blunders and discoveries. The Leavis moral tone takes the measure of everything and keeps a record: one of the features of the Leavis page is the peppering of footnotes that jerk the reader's eye down to past Leavisian pronouncements as if to Holy Writ: "I [F. R. L.] have discussed the force of this phrase of Lawrence's in the note at the end of *D. H. Lawrence: Novelist*, and in the essay on *Anna Karenina* in *Anna Karenina and Other Essays*"; "*V.* my [Q. D. L.'s] introductions and Notes to the Penguin English Library editions of *Jane Eyre* and *Silas Marner* and my essay on *Wuthering Heights* in *Lectures in America* . . ."; or —a fine stroke by Q. D. L.—". . . *v. Anna Karenina and Other Essays*, 'Adam Bede,' where F. R. Leavis discusses . . ." When all is said and done, it was all said and done in the family, and it was always right. Why, then, don't we get more references to past pronouncements on the subject of their new book?

The reason is that they've changed their minds about Dickens. For instance, in the new book's Preface (credited to both authors: but each of the chapters is by one or the other),

"We should like to make it impossible . . . for any intellectual —academic, journalist or both—to tell us with the familiar easy assurance that Dickens of course was a genius, but that his line was entertainment . . ."; while a generation ago, in *The Great Tradition*, Leavis told us with the familiar easy assurance that he had excluded Dickens from "the line of great novelists" because, though "Dickens was a great genius and is permanently among the classics . . . the genius was that of a great entertainer. . . ." In *Dickens the Novelist* Leavis denounces "critics . . . who can tell us . . . that Dickens never grew up intellectually . . ."; while in *The Great Tradition*, exhibiting from an early James novel a (quite commonplace) passage in which "the influence of Dickens is plain," Leavis remarked that "of course" it "couldn't possibly have been written by Dickens: something has been done to give the Dickensian manner a much more formidable intellectual edge," that it "engages mature standards and interest such as Dickens was innocent of"; at another moment in the same book Leavis spoke, as he often does, for "the adult mind," which "doesn't as a rule find in Dickens a challenge to an unusual and sustained seriousness"; and in *Fiction and the Reading Public*, on the same issue, Mrs. Leavis was still more severe—"The peculiarity of Dickens, as any one who runs a critical eye over a novel or two of his can see, is that his originality is confined to recapturing a child's outlook on the grown-up world, emotionally he is not only uneducated but immature." In the same passage she dismissed the figure of Sir Leicester Dedlock as among "the painful guesses of the uninformed and half-educated writing for the uniformed and half-educated"; but in her chapter on *Bleak House* in *Dickens the Novelist* she devotes to Sir Leicester seven pages of enthusiastic analysis, concluding that he "ends in pathos and dignity and is like Gridley in representing the moral courage which in our Chancery world is heroism." In the new book she says that Dickens "gives proof of his understanding that Love as a reality, not a Victorian convention, did inevitably exist"; to the Mrs. Leavis of *Fiction and the Reading Public*, however, "Dickens stands primarily for a set of crude emotional exercises. He discovered . . . the formula 'laughter and tears' that has been the foundation of practically every popular success ever since (Hollywood's as well as the bestseller's). Far from requiring an intellectual stimulus, these are the tears that rise in the heart and gather to the eyes involuntarily or even in spite of the reader, though an alert critical mind may cut them off at the source in a revulsion to disgust" (the function of the "alert critical mind" being to stand guard over every rabbit-hole of feeling, at the ready for the popping out of inappropriate rabbits). The younger Mrs. Leavis compared Dickens unfavorably with Henry Mackenzie! who "at any rate represent[ed] a cultivation of the emotions founded on a gentle code"; now, in her chapter on *David Copperfield*, she compares Dickens with Tolstoy and finds that "they are two similar geniuses of the art of the novel of whom the earlier has the additional prestige of being the great original." The most interesting pair of instances occur in Leavis's essay on *Hard Times*, which, after its first appearance in *Scrutiny*, is reprinted in both *The Great Tradition* and *Dickens the Novelist* with no indication in the latter that the last sentence of the opening paragraph has been substantially changed. The sentence reads now, in a riot of Jamesian commas that tacitly embrace all of Dickens: "Yet, if I am right, of all Dickens's works it is the one that, having the distinctive strength that makes him a major artist, has it in so compact a way, and with a concentrated significance so immediately clear and penetrating, as, one would have thought, to preclude the reader's failing to recognize that he had before him a completely serious, and, in its originality, a triumphantly successful, work of art"; whereas in *The Great Tradition* it was a sober qualification that categorically excluded all of Dickens except *Hard Times:* "Yet, if I am right, of all Dickens's works it is the one that has all the strength of his genius, together with a strength no other of them can show—that of a completely serious work of art." It is interesting, finally, that during twenty-one years *Scrutiny* published two articles on Dickens: one, Leavis's on *Hard Times*; the other, a conventional, unexcited piece by R. C. Churchill that refers, as if to self-evident fact, to such "more important novelists [than Dickens] . . . as George Eliot, Hardy and Conrad."

The point is not that the Leavises haven't the right to change their minds, or that they are disingenuous or dishonest in not letting us know they've changed their minds (surely they understand that not only their hosts of ill-wishers, but puzzled admirers, will recall and connect and wonder); it's that forty years of their insufferable moral tone—"There has been no excuse at any time for any reader not to realize the nature and take the force of this 'social criticism' as . . . [*Little Dorrit*] makes it" (though Leavis himself, as he doesn't say, needed forty years and more)—so many years of this bullying have made it impossible for them to acknowledge anything short of Argus-eyed omniscience. Something like truth, shifty and approximate, becomes as irrelevant as the weather to a space capsule in orbit.

The tone wasn't always so compulsive and disabling, and would sometimes virtually evaporate in the warmth of a congenial poet:

> Poetic creation as the nineteenth century understood it is often in Pope the essential means to a destructive satiric effect. It is so in the passage about Bentley, which is complex and varied in satiric method:
>
> > As many quit the streams that murm'ring fall
> > To lull the sons of Marg'ret and Clare-hall,
> > Where Bentley late tempestuous wont to sport
> > In troubled waters, but now sleeps in Port.
> > Before them march'd that awful Aristarch;
> > Plough'd was his front with many a deep Remark:
> > His Hat, which never vail'd to human pride,
> > Walker with rev'rence took, and laid aside.
> > Low bow'd the rest: He, kingly, did but nod,
> > So upright Quakers please both Man and God.
> > Mistress! dismiss that rabble from your throne:
> > Avaunt—is Aristarchus yet unknown?
> > Thy mighty Scholiast, whose unweary'd pains
> > Made Horace dull, and humbled Milton's strains.
> > Turn what they will to Verse, their toil is vain,
> > Critics like me shall make it Prose again.
>
> The famous pun on Port is a truly poetic pun, depending for its rich effect on the evocative power of the first couplet: the streams are really lulling as if they had been Tennyson's, with

the result that, after "tempestuous," the "troubled waters" are
to the imagination a stormy sea as well as a metaphorical
cliché, and Bentley is both the Leviathan resting in sheltered
waters after majestic play and the befuddled don dozing. The
satiric effect depends upon his being really felt as impressive;
the majesty of the Leviathan is carried over to the "awful Aristarch." The impressiveness suddenly takes on a merely ridiculous aspect when the focus of attention shifts to the impressed:

> His Hat, which never vail'd to human pride,
> Walker with rev'rence took, and laid aside.

—The Vice-Master of Trinity playing the flunkey is comically
absurd, and Bentley becomes merely a comically, if sublimely,
pompous old don. After that the satiric method changes; in
Bentley's speech we are more aware of the ironical satirist than
of the awful Aristarch himself:

> Turn what they will to Verse, their toil is vain,
> Critics like me shall make it Prose again.

This is from *Revaluation*, and here is another passage on Pope:
"Is it necessary to disclaim the suggestion that he is fairly
represented in short extracts? No one, I imagine, willingly
reads through the *Essay on Man* (Pope piquing himself on
philosophical or theological profundity and acumen is intolera-
ble, and he cannot, as Dryden can, argue interestingly in verse);
but to do justice to him one must read through not merely the
Epistles, but, also as a unit, the fourth book of the *Dunciad*,
which I am inclined to think the most striking manifestation of
his genius. It is certainly satire, and I know of nothing that
demonstrates more irresistibly that satire can be great poetry."
Behind the first passage is Empson, behind the second, Eliot;
yet neither could have written this generous statement of
Pope's rank and quality; and *Revaluation* is one of the important books of literary criticism of the century, not only because
it accommodates to its own purposes such innovators as Empson and Eliot, but because it offers the first coherent and plausible twentieth-century account of the English poetic tradition.

By the time Leavis arrives at Dickens, however, even the
desire to praise doesn't help:

We have here, representatively manifest, the impersonalizing
process of Dickens's art: the way in which he has transmuted his

personal experience into something that is not personal, but felt by us as reality and truth presented, for what with intrinsic authority they are, by impersonal intelligence. His essential social criticism doesn't affect us as urged personally by the writer. It has the disinterestedness of spontaneous life, undetermined and undirected and uncontrolled by idea, will and self-insistent ego, the disinterestedness here being that which brings a perceived significance to full realization and completeness in art. The writer's labour has been to present something that speaks for itself.

The last sentence is the annihilating commentary on all that precedes it. Veteran readers of Leavis will recognize the old code-words—"reality and truth," "intrinsic authority," "spontaneous life," "perceived significance"—but will be reluctant to grant that they were ever in the past used with such unevocative inertness, in such paraplegic cadences.

An unpsychiatric explanation of the difference between Leavis on Pope and Leavis on Dickens is that Leavis's critical procedure (like Eliot's) was developed and most effectively exerted in the study of poetry. The procedure, rooted in the altogether reasonable assumption that particular words and phrases count for almost everything in a literary work, emphasizes close analysis of representative extracts; but it's a procedure more sympathetic to poetry than to prose fiction, which is less localizable because it functions over much longer spans of attention toward much more mixed and more complicated effects. When Leavis began dealing with fiction on an ambitious scale, in the pieces which were eventually gathered into *The Great Tradition*, it became clear that he had met an unanticipated problem of evidence. He seemed to sense the problem, but showed no sign of learning how to cope with it, as his citations swelled into more and more numerous and grossly unwieldy "extracts," to which he would append efforts at close analysis that were usually defeated not only by the size of the extracts but by the refractory nature of fiction. Most of the time what he said appeared to have little to do with what he had quoted. He tended to settle into book-reviewer bosh, of the sort that culminates in *Dickens the Novelist:* "profound insight into human nature," "the infinitely varied power of his prose," "the inexhaustible subtlety of the greatest art," "consummate art," "cogent felicity," and—telltale compliment, when everything else seemed inadequate—"a great poet who is essentially a novelist" (has Leavis inadvertently reversed the nouns?), "Dickens the poet, the incomparable Victorian master of poetic expression" (all these from a few pages of the chapter on *Little Dorrit*). His style began to fail in its responsiveness to metaphor ("From the utilitarian schoolroom Mr. Gradgrind walks toward his utilitarian abode, Stone Lodge, which, as Dickens evokes it, brings home to us concretely . . ."), began to lose its (in any case limited) flexibility, and became characteristically—what it could always be in fits of Leavisian grandeur—tremulous, fussy, abstract, not deliberate but dogmatic, punctuated by irritable assertions of authority. So Mrs. Leavis, taking up the family burden, insists that "the rewritten end [of *Great Expectations*] is demonstrably superior," and "the idea now sedulously propaganded [*sic*] that Dickens's characters make merely theatrical gestures and facial signs is demonstrably false." Immodest and powerless, the critic daydreams about producing mathematical proofs out of his pocket and pigeons out of his armpit.

Or, baffled by the loss of his ability to persuade, he conjures up a good old time when it was only necessary for authority to stand benignly by while the lower orders occupied themselves with fertility festivals and the rising middle class with close reading. What the Leavises, having renounced criticism, are now intent on celebrating is the Golden Age, such as Mrs. Leavis tried to recollect it in *Fiction and the Reading Public:* those halcyon days before the coming of the mawkish, uninformed, uneducated Dickens (in the newly revised version of the myth, Dickens is slipped in as the glorious climactic exemplar of the Age), when in the cities every reader pored over edifying, mind-stretching books and journals, and (as Leavis reminds us in his chapter on *Dombey and Son*) out in the suburbs, among the sinewy English workers and peasants, "the humble, populous and happy home of the Toodles family . . . stand[s] for that which is repressed and denied by the Dombey code: human kindness, natural human feeling, thriving human life." (According to Leavis, characters in fiction—"Sissy stands for vitality as well as goodness"—always "stand for" something or other: the guileless allegorizing is probably another habit left over from his earlier concentration on poetry, in which words are more likely to give the unwary reader an impression of relatively unimpeded symbolic resonances.) As one would expect of such unappeasable traditionalists, the villains of their book are those criminal idiots who try to make do with the present, i.e., all the rest of the extant population of the English-speaking world, especially Americans: "In our Kingsley-Amis type civilization 'delicacy' has become a term of contempt with the intellectual guardians of our culture"; ". . . in the opinion of the more recent trans-Atlantic thesis-writers (there is always a smart Dickens book in vogue with the academics and literary journalists, and those favoured at the moment seem to be Garis and Dabney) . . ."; "the Holloways of Eng. Lit." (John Holloway, who unlike the Leavises—the Murdstones of Lit. Crit.—is not plural, had ventured to publish an essay in respectful disagreement with Leavis's on *Hard Times*); "[Dickens] . . . is very often less simple-minded than his critics, especially those outside the English tradition and in such a brutally crude one as the modern American"; "To those troubled by the vanishing of what humanity more and more desperately needs if it is not to be deprived of all that makes it human . . ."; ". . . anyone who is now engaged in reading English Literature with undergraduates even in England must feel (unless of the same generation) that he has to introduce delicately complex perceptions and a social civilization of which that literature is the flower, to a brutally callous generation as to sensibility, students who except in rare cases have lost contact with the traditional culture . . ."; and—Mrs. Leavis's karate-chop in the groin of a trans-Atlantic critic who was only clearing his throat—"Perhaps a Victorian gentleman's view of having such a patron attached to him as father and house-mate cannot really be understood nowadays, particularly in a country that has accepted violence as a way of life . . ."

There is no end of embarrassments in the book, some familiar, some new. One of Mrs. Leavis's hobby-horses, as far back as her aborted book on Jane Austen, has been to "document" the events of a novel from the life of its author: about Dickens, now, she reveals that his sister "Fanny had played an important part in . . . [his] childhood (even as Florence did to little Paul [Dombey]) and her death contributed to the genuine feeling conveyed [in *David Copperfield*] in the death of David's mother." Having proved to her own satisfaction that a novelist (quite like one of those brutally American Method actors) needs to rake over his private miseries in order to work up a few pages of "genuine feeling," Mrs. Leavis doesn't scruple to initiate us into a yet higher stage of documentation: "Dickens has been scolded by critics for 'not seeing David's first marriage from the woman's (Dora's) point of view,'" but—let's look at the evidence—". . . it is interesting that we *have* the woman's point of view on the same situation and that it rather surprisingly turns out to be essentially identical with Dickens's. . . . In *The Tortoise and the Hare* (1954) an able woman novelist, Miss Elizabeth Jenkins, shows . . ." that, believe it or not, Dickens knows as much about women as Miss Elizabeth Jenkins does. As if all this were not enough, Mrs. Leavis writes the worst sentence in a very badly written book: "For fortunately Dickens was not only a genius as a novelist, he was also a gifted editor and had an intuitive as well as an informed understanding of the problems of providing a diverse and even largely semi-literate and illiterate public with, not something it would have no effort to absorb as entertainment, but with what he himself wanted to write yet which must be presented in a form that such a mixed readership could cope with and get *something* out of—if not all that there was in it to get." Leavis himself, however gallantly he tries, can't match anything so derailed and frantic as that, though he contrives an occasional superlatively leaden sentence of the code-word kind that reads like articulate catatonia: "Actually, the Dickensian vitality is there in its varied characteristic modes, which should—surely —here be the more immediately and perceptively responded to as the agents of a felt compelling significance because they are free of anything that might be seen as redundance: the creative exuberance is controlled by a profound inspiration that informs, directs and limits."

Poor Dickens, when they finish with him, is labels from head to foot. People who sneer at "trans-Atlantic thesis-writers" shouldn't live in glass word-boxes. What the Leavises, speaking up for England, make of Dickens is their own collection of themes and theses as blank as the Leavisian code-words. Nothing much has to be noticed about the good characters except that they all stand for life, "vitality as well as goodness," disinterestedness, "the spontaneous, the real, the creative," "ego-free love," culture, civilization, tradition; all the bad characters stand for you know what; Dickens and the Leavises come out for the former, as Leopold Bloom came out for the opposite of hate. Nothing much, either, has to be noticed about failures of execution and texture, local discrepancies. Thus Mrs. Leavis pursues her thesis that *Great Expectations* is a "schematic novel" for which Dickens produces "the right, because the logical, solution to the problem of how to end without a sentimental 'happy ending' but with a satisfactory winding up of the themes "; and she has no trouble welcoming Dickens's "logical solution"— for the sake of which he discarded his superbly terse first ending and almost spoiled a great novel—welcoming this detritus of Victorian tics, tones, rhythms, repetitions, East-Lynne stage-sets, and sexual unspeakableness:

> The freshness of her beauty was indeed gone, but its indescribable majesty and its indescribable charm remained. . . .
>
> We sat down on a bench that was near, and I said, "After so many years, it is strange that we should thus meet again, Estella, here where our first meeting was! Do you often come back?"
>
> "I have never been here since."
>
> "Nor I."
>
> The moon began to rise, and I thought of the placid look at the white ceiling, which had passed away. The moon began to rise, and I thought of the pressure on my hand when I had spoken the last words he had heard on earth.
>
> Estella was the next to break the silence that ensued between us.

But neither does Mrs. Leavis blush to write that *Great Expectations* is "seriously engaged in discussing, by exemplifying, profound and basic realities of human experience."

This profound and basic English, though thank God it isn't the language of Dickens the novelist, is the language of *Dickens the Novelist*. This is what remains of Leavis and company; but Leavis—in a way so special, so thoroughly assimilated into the body of contemporary critical practice, that bright young academics are hard put to understand why they owe him anything—was a distinguished critic and, even more, an exemplary literary figure at a time when the Anglo-American academy was confidently driving to establish for all time the difference between literary scholarship and mere criticism (the latter being to the former what jellybeans are to steak and potatoes). The academy could have neutralized the chameleon Eliot and the eccentric Empson, it could and did annex the genteel Brookses, Tates, Ransoms; but it couldn't fend off Leavis, who knew all the academic dirty tricks from the inside, was a pedant himself and the scourge of pedants, thrived on ostracism, remembered and extravagantly repaid all insults, triumphed not less by his malicious pleasure in crushing the stupid and infamous than by his appreciative intelligence. *Scrutiny* gave up the ghost in 1953: that was already at least a decade after Leavis had had anything new to say. He had won the war, but, victim of the spleen that had nerved him to fight it, was himself its most eminent and most depressing casualty.

VII.
Saint-Simon

Saint-Simon[1] is certainly the great memorialist of peculiar behavior, never hesitating to interrupt his narrative with page after page of descriptions of tics and quirks. The Marquise de Saint-Hérem, for instance, "once succeeded in boiling her own leg in the middle of the River Seine, near Fontainebleau. The water had proved too cold for her liking when she was bathing, and she had had large quantities heated on the bank and poured around and over her, with the result that she was severely scalded and remained housebound for a week. In thunderstorms she had a habit of going down on all fours under her day-bed, and obliging her servants to be piled on top of her, so that the thunder might lose its effect before it reached her." When the Comte de Gramont "was 85 and mortally ill his wife tried to speak to him of God"; his busy life, however, had left him no time for religion, and "when she had finished he said, 'But, Madame, is what you say really true?' When he heard her recite the Paternoster he said 'I think that is a beautiful prayer, who wrote it?' " The Duc de Chevreuse, a man who couldn't be hurried (and therefore didn't spare the horses),

---

[1]Lucy Norton (ed.), *Historical Memoirs of the Duc de Saint-Simon*, Vol. I (New York, 1967); Vol. II (New York, 1968); Vol. III (New York, 1972).

> . . . used sometimes to keep his horses standing harnessed for twelve or fifteen hours at a time. One morning, at Vaucresson, he had decided to dine at Dampierre. The coachman first, then the postillion, grew tired holding the horses' heads. This was in the summer. By six in the evening, even the horses were bored. There ensued a tremendous noise that set the house shaking. Everyone rushed out. They found the coach in fragments, the great door of the house splintered, the garden gate that enclosed one side of the courtyard battered down, in short, complete destruction which it took a very long time to repair. M. de Chevreuse, quite oblivious of all the commotion, was much surprised when he learned what had happened. . . .

The Duc de Vivonne had little to do with his wife and wasn't on speaking terms with his son; but "when the son lay dying, M. de Vivonne was shamed into visiting him. He found him *in extremis* but did not approach, merely stood leaning against a table calmly observing him. The entire family were present lamenting. After a prolonged silence M. de Vivonne suddenly took it into his head to remark: 'Poor fellow! He will not recover. I remember seeing his father die in just the same way.' You may imagine the scandal caused by those words, the supposed father being one of M. de Vivonne's grooms. M. de Vivonne himself appeared quite unperturbed, and after another silence left the room." The Marquis de Reffuge "was highly respectable, and sober, but vastly absent-minded. His valets sometimes took advantage of that fact to bring him at one time seven or eight glasses of wine, none of which he had ordered, and he would swallow all of them without thinking. Thus he was frequently drunk, and when he came to his senses could never imagine how it had happened." The Duke of Alba, a very old and eminent counselor to the King of Spain, was discovered by a French visitor

> . . . in a somewhat filthy state, on his right side between two sheets, where he had been for months past without changing his position or allowing them to make his bed. He said he had no strength to get up; yet his health was excellent. The fact was that he was in despair because his mistress had grown tired of him and had left him. He had sent out parties to search for her throughout the whole of Spain, and, such is piety in countries of

the Inquisition, had had masses and prayers said in the churches
for her return. Finally he had taken this vow to remain in bed
without shifting off his right side until she was recaptured. . . .
Many visitors called to see him, some of them of the highest
birth, for he was good company. With that vow to hamper him
he was unable to play any part at the death of Charles II or at
the accession of Philip V, whom he never saw despite his protes-
tations of loyalty. He carried on in this absurd fashion until the
day he died, never leaving his bed nor turning off his right
side. . . ..

Such tidbits suggest that the seventeenth-century high no-
bility, free to do almost anything, are liable to do almost anything: idiosyncrasies pop up in every unexpected shape and
size, and Saint-Simon welcomes them all with generous enthusiasm. Where comment isn't called for, Saint-Simon doesn't
offer any; but the vignette about the Spanish duke is more
complex than the others because it touches on two issues—
piety and political responsibility—that call for comment from a
serious man.

Saint-Simon is a good French Catholic, partisan of "the
Gallican Church" and enemy of "the ultramontane principle"
of Papal supremacy; convinced that human authority must be
plural, that the diffusion and localization of authority are as essential to religious as to political order; for whom the Pope is
doubtless the Bishop of Rome and otherwise a parvenu ambitious for the rôle of autocrat of Christendom; a rational
Frenchman horrified by the Inquisition and contemptuous of
the claptrap of superstition with which the Spanish clergy keep
their flock at heel; whose perfect confidence in distinguishing
right from wrong doesn't admit the intimation that religion and
reason may sometimes be at odds. Saint-Simon makes clear
that a piety compatible with behavior as sinful and preposterous as the Duke of Alba's isn't worthy of the name ("such is
piety in countries of the Inquisition"); that a nobleman who
allows a fit of absurdity to disable him for his important political office is not only absurd but reprehensible. Yet Saint-
Simon notes that the Duke "was good company"; notes the
fact of his despair (and the antecedent fact of his passion); is
fascinated by still another testimony to the boundlessness of

human possibility: "This was such extraordinary behaviour," he concludes, "and so clearly proved that I thought it worth mentioning of a man who in all other ways was sensible and intelligent."

Saint-Simon isn't a taxonomist of the trivial, he isn't ever a cynic or a skeptic or even a wit (though he is often marvelously witty). He isn't the Anglo-American reader's favorite uncle, that dilettante and pyrrhonist the cultivated Frenchman (somebody like, say, Stendhal or Proust, each of whom regarded himself as a disciple of Saint-Simon's), though his epigrams may in isolation make him for a moment now and then seem so: "nothing upsets a cardinal"; "Mme Tencin and her brother the abbé were one in heart and soul, if they may be said to have possessed either"; "He passed among fools for being a man of sense." But Saint-Simon's epigrams aren't oblique and catty, fired on the run, intended to muddle and derange the will; on the contrary they serve his rage for clarity, for exact and complete definition, for the structure of truth bristling with qualifications:

> Bezons was a commoner, a coarse and brutal fellow who had run away from the parental home when his father wished to make a priest of him. He enlisted as an ordinary soldier in a body of troops going secretly to Portugal, and fought there in the ranks. His father's inquiries soon established his identity; he was promoted, and served with keenness and industry. The Latin which he learned before joining was all the education he ever received, but he none the less became a good general, especially skilful at manoeuvring a wing of cavalry. His rudeness, however, and his evil temper often prevented him from seeing other men's points of view. All in all, he was a man with much personal courage, not unfamiliar with the idea of honour, but always at a loss, very diffident, a trimmer, with a great desire to arrive and make a fortune. He was also vastly mean and vastly boring, not entirely devoid of commonsense, with a small talent for intrigues of short duration, and possessed of a fairly sound judgment. He had a leonine head of huge dimensions and blubber-lips, the whole surrounded by an immense wig, which would have made him a good model for Rembrandt, and looked all of a piece with his great body. He passed among fools for being a man of sense. . . .

This force, assurance, headlong straightforwardness, candor; the colloquial and asymmetrical ease of the phrasing (from a *Grand-Siècle* chronicler who records the deaths of his contemporaries La Fontaine, Boileau, Racine); the indifference to tidiness and mere consistency; the absolute fidelity to a single point of view without spite or malice—they are all characteristic Saint-Simon. Bezons is one of the more obscure among the thousands of men and women whom, during thirty-two years at the French Court, Saint-Simon knew and committed to his journal in a storm of epithets and anecdotes that, chronological centuries and political millennia later, continue to strike with the velocity and distinctness of hailstones. The *Memoirs* were unpublished and virtually unknown in Saint-Simon's lifetime, they couldn't otherwise have been written; but the energy they radiate is unconditional, and nothing seems more unlikely than the fact that they were private papers.

The *Memoirs* include everything (for instance, they have more first-family genealogies than the Bible), and they are far less episodic than they appear to be in samplings. Even idiosyncrasy isn't merely Saint-Simon's comic relief, indeed it fascinates him because he considers it the secret spring that moves or stops the world; it accounts not only for the Duke of Alba's dirty sheets but for the rise and fall of empires. According to Saint-Simon, everybody freely chooses to do what he does, which is often strange enough to prevent him from ever again finding the way back to simplicity, love, and reason; kings and princes freely choose the traps into which they permit themselves to be driven, and empires fall. The Duc d'Orléans, Saint-Simon's lifelong friend, an intelligent, likable, complicated, and not wholly corrupted man, Regent of France after Louis XIV's death, commits moral suicide by choosing as his principal adviser the odious Abbé Dubois: "All the vices fought for mastery in . . . [Dubois]. Avarice, debauchery, ambition were his gods; treachery, flattery, subservience, his expedients." But decades ago, in his childhood, the Duke had had Dubois thrust upon him, as his tutor. But the Duke might have escaped if he had not himself chosen to live a debauched life that weakened and eventually destroyed his capacity for resisting wickedness in others. Dubois, not yet a priest, demands to be made Archbishop of Cambrai. Exclaims the Regent scornfully: "You, Archbishop of Cambrai! A man like you!" Dubois insists, and quotes precedents of other (as Saint-Simon calls them) "vermin, eccentrics, and perverts" without vocation or previous experience appointed to high clerical posts. "M. le Duc d'Orléans was shaken; less by such hollow arguments than by his inability to stand against a man whom he dared not even contradict. He tried to escape by exclaiming, 'You shark! Where will you ever find another willing to consecrate you?' 'Oh!' said Dubois, 'if that is all, the deed is as good as done; for there is a man in the next room who will be glad to officiate.' " And bounds into the next room from which he plucks the Bishop of Nantes, who does the deed. Within a year he is in correspondence with Rome to be made cardinal. The Regent, having been informed,

> . . . burst out laughing. "Cardinal!" he cried, "that little worm! You must be joking, he would never dare." And when Torcy showed him proof, he lost his temper, exclaiming that if Master Impudence had any such notion, he would clap him into a deep dungeon. He several times repeated that phrase, in fact whenever Torcy produced fresh evidence, from foreign letters, of the continuing intrigue. On the last occasion, when the hat was almost won, Torcy heard the same words repeated with equal fury. Yet when he visited the Regent next day, at the Palais Royal, M. le Duc d'Orléans beckoned him into a corner to say, "By the way, Monsieur, please write to Rome in my name, requesting a hat for Monsieur de Cambrai. Do not delay, speed is essential."

A year later, having heard that Dubois is about to be made first minister, Saint-Simon visits the Regent: "he looked worried and abstracted, and indeed he asked me several times to repeat myself—he, whose mind was ordinarily far ahead of mine, who loved to joke on the gravest matters, especially with me, saying outrageous things to try my patience, and then bursting into laughter because I always got angry." Saint-Simon is full of affection, pity, concern, and, as usual, the best and lengthiest advice: "He had only one thing to do, I continued, prefer good to bad in every kind. . . . Let him reflect that his present ways became disgraceful after the age of eighteen or twenty. The racket, the language devoid of all decency, were utterly degrading, while drunkenness effectively banished any last shred of dignity or good breeding that might still cling to him. . . . I ended by entreating him to remember that for years past I had said nothing of his personal conduct. I should not mention it now had he not forced me by showing me the awful abyss into which he would fall, if boredom alone drove him to appointing a first minister." The Regent listens, makes a joke or two, confesses to his old friend that he has "lost all desire for women," agrees that Dubois is as bad as can be. The next day Saint-Simon reappears renewing the siege with volleys of unanswerable arguments and horrid historical examples, to which again the Regent listens till at last "he turned towards me without raising his eyes, and in a low, unhappy voice exclaimed, 'We cannot go on like this; he must be appointed at once.' " So Dubois becomes prime minister and the *de facto* ruler of France.

Saint-Simon denies that it all had to happen. He is as thorough a voluntarist as possible, in his actions at Court as well as in the pages of the *Memoirs:* he keeps resisting wicked men and supporting the good or at least the well-intentioned, keeps believing that the light of reason can penetrate the self-deception of kings and princes, never surrenders, keeps hurrying up and down the corridors seizing and rattling the bars of all the cages. (Once, though, for a moment, his spirit almost fails and, as he contemplates twenty-four years of an honest courtier's disappointments and disasters culminating in the untimely death of the prince who might have been not the great but the good king of France, he is compelled to admit that "I found it very hard not to despair.") He is quite Promethean, challenging the heavens for the sake of justice and his beloved France; but he manages to avoid retribution—he would have out-talked if not out-wrestled any avenging angel sent to fetch him—and survives by many years the events of his epic narrative.

The *Memoirs* have a subject, nothing less than the destiny of France; and three tragic protagonists: Louis XIV, the Duc de Bourgogne, and the Duc d'Orléans. Louis is of course the grandest and the most fully considered. For Saint-Simon he is not the good but the great king of France: he has already reigned for forty-eight years and ruled autocratically for thirty when Saint-Simon comes to Versailles in 1691; he is the Sun King, whose bright or clouded face determines place and fortune; by the time of his death in the seventy-third year of his reign he is the only imaginable king (when his pages wept at his deathbed he said, "Why are you crying? Did you think I was immortal?"). Because the nobles had attempted a rebellion against him when he was the child-king, he would never learn to trust them. As soon as he had the power he set about eroding their ceremonies, their prerogatives, their independence, their advisory influence, their pride; built Versailles to keep them out of mischief away from their estates and under his observant eye competing for his favors; reserved political office and advancement for commoners who owed him everything and whom he could unmake with a word, men who had "the one essential quality without which no man could, nor ever did, enter the council of Louis XIV during his entire reign (save only for M. de Beauvilliers), viz., a total lack of breeding."

Because his bastards too have the luck of owing him everything, he grants them unprecedented status at Court; toward the end of his life even dares establish them by proclamation in the line of succession to the throne; obliges the legitimate children of the royal family, as well as his royal cousins the Princes of the Blood, to accept them in marriage till it would take Aquinas to judge the degree and propriety of the relationships all ascending to Louis as if to Father Adam. For example, Louis obliges the young Duc de Chartres (later Duc d'Orléans), the son of Louis's brother, to marry Louis's bastard daughter and therefore the Duke's first cousin Mlle. de Blois. Eighteen years later their daughter (Louis's granddaughter-grandniece) is deemed by Louis suitable for marriage with one of his legitimate grandsons the Duc de Berry, the young couple therefore sharing the King as their grandfather. (Louis seems to have thought that closing the family circle was as important as cementing foreign alliances by royal marriages: he enjoyed having lots of company at Versailles and Marly, and he felt more comfortable with blood-relatives.)

For an autocrat, Louis is a surprisingly devious, in-decisive, anxious man. Incapable of dismissing anyone directly from court or from a governmental or military post, he signals his loss of confidence by a repertoire of snubs intended to break the victim's spirit (but, comically, ineffective with a trou-blemaker and thorn in the side as resolute as Saint-Simon, who is always ready to reinstate himself by drawing the King into a catechism of air-clearing and getting-down-to-cases as between indulgent father and respectful son). If confrontation is unevad-able, the King prefers that it be one to one: perhaps because of his memory of the rebellion a half-century earlier, he "feared and disliked anything smacking of a concerted action," so that, for instance, if the dukes wish to approach him on an issue of ducal privilege, it will never do for more than one of them at a time to seek an audience with him. Nor does he like to make decisions concerning the various factions at Court that are jockeying for advantage: he stalls and temporizes, and seems really uneasy and distressed to be caught in the middle. He insists on the courtiers' presence daily as a mark of their submission ("I do not see him," says the haughty King, ex-pressing his displeasure with one nobleman or another who isn't continuously visible at Versailles through the four sea-sons), he won't delegate the most trifling judgment on protocol, he insists on holding and, when pressed, exercising all power; but his insistence lacks the tyrannical relish, so that his monop-oly of power seems, if not just a habit, a consequence of his fear of powerlessness; he is the chief clerk in this Kafkan pal-ace of mirrors. No doubt things were different in his heyday, and Saint-Simon, coming on the scene after a half-century's reign, has missed much: the many mistresses; the successful wars; great ministers and soldiers like Colbert and Turenne; the great writers. Now Corneille and Molière are dead, fol-lowed in the early years of Saint-Simon's chronicle by La Fon-taine, Boileau, Racine; the wars go badly; the ministers are flunkeys, unequal to the burden of a nearly bankrupt war econ-omy; the King himself is a miracle of longevity, his person and manner more and more majestic and awe-inspiring, but rather a prig and a conventional Papist under the influence of Mme. de Maintenon (his legal but officially unacknowledged wife), his Jesuit confessors, and his old age. Cabals form, gain ascendancy, are on the verge of triumph, collapse with the sudden deaths of their leaders or figureheads, and the years pass in the claustrophobia of Versailles as it seems more and more likely that the King, lacking any other conspicuous virtues, is only omnipotent and immortal.

All of the King's feelings in his old age are mortgaged and encumbered—except the pleasure he takes in his granddaughter-in-law (and grandniece) the Duchesse de Bourgogne: "an adorable princess," says Saint-Simon,

> . . . whose gracious charm and kindness had so completely captured the hearts of the King, Mme de Maintenon, and Mgr le Duc de Bourgogne that even their extreme vexation with her father the Duke of Savoy could not lessen their delight in her. The King kept no secrets from her, worked in her presence with his ministers, and was careful for her sake not to speak against her father when she was within hearing. When they were alone she would jump on to his knee kissing and hugging him, and with pretty teasing ways rummage through his papers, opening and reading his letters[2] (sometimes against his will) and treating Mme de Maintenon much the same. Yet she never made mischief for anyone, indeed she was kind to all and softened the blows whenever she could do so. She was considerate of the King's servants, even the humblest, gentle with her own household, and lived on terms of easy intimacy with all her ladies, young and old. She was the life and light of the Court; every one adored and lived to please her. When she was not there everything seemed flat and dull; her presence enlivened all the pleasures.

In 1711 the torpid and mean-spirited Monseigneur, heir to the throne, quite suddenly dies. The Duc de Bourgogne, whom Saint-Simon already reveres and whose friend and adviser he will soon become, is Dauphin; one of the new Dauphine's intimates is Mme. de Saint-Simon. It is Saint-Simon's *annus mirabilis*. One evening the Dauphine, amusing the King with

---

[2]From which she did not scruple to transmit information to her father. The King found out ("The little wretch has betrayed us!" he exclaimed), but he didn't mend either his ways or hers.

her usual airy nonsense, notices disdainful looks from the ladies of the late Monseigneur's cabal:

As soon as the King had risen and moved to his inner study to
feed his dogs, the Dauphine seized Mme de Saint-Simon and
Mme de Levis by the hand, and pointing to those princesses,
only a few feet away, cried: "Did you see them? Did you see
them? I know as well as they do that I behave absurdly and
must seem very silly; but he needs to have a bustle about him
and that kind of thing amuses him." Then, swinging on their
arms, she began to laugh and sing, "Ha-ha! it makes me laugh,
Ha-ha! I can laugh at them, because I shall be their queen. I
need not mind them now or ever, but they will have to reckon
with me, for I shall be their queen," and she shouted and sang
and hopped and laughed as high and as loud as she dared. Mme
de Saint-Simon and Mme de Levis whispered to her to be quiet
lest the princesses should hear her, and the entire company
think that she had taken leave of her senses, but she only
skipped and sang the more, "What do I care for them? I'm
going to be their queen!" and so she continued until the King's
return. Alas! sweet princess, she believed what she said, and
who could have thought otherwise? But for our sins it pleased
God very shortly to arrange matters differently.

In a few months she is dead at 26. "With her death all joy
vanished, all pleasures, diversions and delights were overcast,
and darkness covered the Court"; and Saint-Simon adds, with
a perhaps pardonable lapse into the clairvoyance of fiction,
that "The King and Mme de Maintenon were penetrated with
the most violent grief, the only real grief which he ever experienced." A week later her husband is dead also (in that awful
year for the King, not only his special darling but three of his
heirs—his son, his grandson, and his great-grandson—die: conspiracy and poison are suspected; but nothing is ever proved);
and with the Dauphin, as Saint-Simon believes, dies the hope
of France:

The noble and most Christian precept that kings are made for
their peoples, not peoples for their kings, was so firmly implant-
ed in his heart that splendour and war were hateful to him. It
thus happened that he sometimes argued too forcibly against
war; he was carried away by truths too hard for the ears of

worldly men, and on that account people often said maliciously that he was afraid to fight. His justice was blindfolded with all the thoroughness that safety requires. He carefully studied every case that came to the King for judgment at the various councils, and if any great matter were involved, he worked with the experts, consulting their opinions, but not slavishly adopting them. . . . He perfectly understood the King, respected him always, and, towards the end, loved him as a son should do. He paid him homage as his subject, but always retained a proper sense of his own rank. . . . He loved his brothers tenderly and his wife with passion. His grief at losing her broke his heart, and only by a most prodigious effort did his religion survive the blow. It was a sacrifice which he offered without reserves and it killed him; yet in his terrible affliction he showed nothing mean nor common, nothing unworthy. . . .

These virtues of moderation and self-constraint he had had to notice and learn and choose; for he

. . . was born with a violent temper and in his early youth had been terrifying. Hard and choleric to the last degree, subject to transports of rage even against inanimate objects, furiously impetuous, unable to brook the slightest opposition, even from time or the weather, without flying into a passion that seemed likely to destroy his entire body, he was stubborn beyond measure, mad for all kinds of amusement, a woman-lover and at the same time, which is rare, with an equally strong propensity in another direction. He loved wine and good eating just as much, was passionately fond of hunting and listened to music in a kind of ecstasy. Cards delighted him, but he so hated to lose that it was dangerous to play against him. In sum, he was a prey to all the passions and loved all pleasures. . . .

Saint-Simon sees him for the last time soon after the Dauphine's death: ". . . he neither moved nor spoke. . . . I dared to take him by the arm, saying that he must sooner or later see the King, who was waiting for him and must be longing to embrace him, and that it would therefore be kind not to delay. Then, gently urging him to start, I took the liberty of giving him a little push. He gave me such a look as nearly broke my heart and immediately left the room. I followed him a little way and then went to recover myself. I never saw him again."

Within a week on his own deathbed, knowing that he is dying, the Dauphin chooses a death of piety and peace:

Such thankfulness he expressed that he was not required to reign and render an account of kingship! How humble, how excellent he was! How truly he loved God! How clearly he saw his own sins and unworthiness! How modest his hopes! How peaceful his mind! How marvellous his understanding of God's mercy! How holy his fears! How long he read and prayed; how eagerly received the Last Sacraments! How deep his self-questioning! How invincible his patience; how kind, how considerate he was to all who approached him! In his death France suffered her final punishment, when God disclosed to her the prince whom she did not deserve. Earth was not worthy of him; he was already ripe for the joys of Paradise.

Saint-Simon carried the *Memoirs* forward through the events of another eleven years, till the end of the Regency; he worked on them through most of the rest of his long life, and their power is unaffected by the death of his hope. Like the Dauphin of his exalted peroration, he was a painstaking, responsible man. He had a loving and gracious wife who advised and comforted him, and who as he said "made his life's happiness"; the best among the courtiers sought his friendship, and never broke with him once he gave it. (He was a tiny man, this fiery particle, this "butt-end" as the Court wits dubbed him, wearing the highest heels—they were red too—at Court. He had no luck with his children. His two sons were dull and unpromising, and he did what he could to obtain honorable positions for them. His daughter was so hideously deformed that the Saint-Simons assumed she would never marry: nonetheless a noble but almost ruined suitor, who thought that Saint-Simon's influence with the Regent might accomplish wonders for him, insisted on marrying her over her father's explicit denial—"in his usual emphatic manner," reports a contemporary—that he would ever intervene in any official matter on behalf of a member of his family.) The King, who could hardly have been unaware of Saint-Simon's frequent, forceful, and outspoken disagreement with much that he did and allowed to be done, learned after years of suspicion and coldness to re-

spect him: worried about the bad company that the Duc d'Orléans was keeping, the King remarked that "M. de Saint-
Simon is a good friend of my nephew; I wish he had no other,
for he is an honest man, and always gives him good advice. I
am never anxious on that account. I only wish he did not
follow the advice of others." Saint-Simon was an active, medi-
tative, and observant man, as continuous in all three aspects as
if contradiction were unthinkable among them: no question of
affection or policy inhibited his sense of principle; no question
of principle inhibited his attention to what was actually going
on. He had scores of close and loving friendships, and never betrayed them or was compromised by them. In concert with
others or alone, he acted on his convictions. His fearlessness
and probity were acknowledged even by his enemies, who de-
plored them as dangerous self-indulgences. He was the conscience of the Court, the faithful Kent and Horatio of Louis's
tormented kingdom, and he lived to tell the story.

VIII.
Conrad

Both these books[1] are catalogues of inference and not very carefully hedged speculation, raids on whole libraries of secondary sources, and as smug as people who do forty minutes of calisthenics daily: "Reconstructing the events of the assassination has not been easy, but it has been worthwhile in that it allows us to study an example of Conrad's technique. . . ." All such literary scholarship (the prototype is Lowes's *The Road to Xanadu*) depends on two assumptions: (1) that the author and works being examined are unassailably immortal; and (2) that the method helps us to retrace the steps by which imagination transmutes the dross of experience into the massy gold of art. Somehow, though, the scholar turns out to be the hero. Everybody knows that artists, unlike scholars, are liable to spells of slackness: "The South American continent had been well observed and written about, and Conrad might have put himself through an intensive reading course in preparation for writing . . . [*Nostromo*], had he wished"; but the lengths to which Professor Sherry will go are limited only by his eyesight, as he proves at this point with a great casual one-liner of a

---

[1]Norman Sherry, *Conrad's Eastern World* (Cambridge, 1966); Norman Sherry, *Conrad's Western World* (Cambridge, 1971).

footnote: "I read about 200 books on the area in search of Conrad's sources." Sherry considers a dozen or so novels and stories besides *Nostromo* (multiply 200 by a dozen, and divide by two detached retinas). A scholar who doesn't even trust information (". . . little is known about these men, . . . and, as I shall show, not all the information we have about them is correct . . .") certainly has to burn the midnight oil to keep up. Sherry seems to have devoured not merely all the books but all the newspapers, weeklies, monthlies, pamphlets, manifestoes, court records, official documents, company files, ship's logs, memoirs, diaries of the period between 1880 and 1910 in Singapore, London, the Congo; he interviewed participants, friends of participants, children and grandchildren of participants; he collected photographs:

> . . . at least one assessor described by Conrad in *Lord Jim* approximates in appearance to one of the assessors who sat in judgment over Captain Beard and Conrad in the case of the *Palestine.* " 'Did you think it likely from the force of the blow?' asked the assessor sitting to the left. He had a thin horseshoe beard, salient cheek-bones, and with both elbows on the desk clasped his rugged hands before his face . . ." (p. 33). This is the same assessor described above as a "sailing-ship skipper with a reddish beard" and a "pious disposition." I have a photograph in my possession of John Blair, one of the nautical assessors in the *Palestine* Inquiry. He is a man of strong appearance, noticeable cheek-bones and a thin horseshoe beard. Blair was not, at the time of the *Palestine* Court of Inquiry, a "sailing-ship skipper" but he had been some six years previously, before his vessel was wrecked off Raffles Lighthouse, Singapore.

Such triumphantly circumstantial correspondences! but "So what?" snarls Reader X, unwilling to cry uncle or captain at the reduplicated horseshoe beard or any other scrap of false specification. Does Sherry (or Conrad) think a real beard or a Captain Beard is no bristlier than a mere fictional beard?[2] Life

---

[2]In the chapter on Lawrence, you met Harry T. Moore worrying abut Lawrence's non-fictional beard and Birkin beardless.

doesn't slide over into fiction so readily as that, but Sherry hasn't noticed.

One of the drawbacks of his method is that, spending eons at it, digging up beards and cheekbones, he doesn't see why it shouldn't explain how novels are put together or come apart: "There is a change in the character of the hero in *Lord Jim* once he goes to Patusan. This change is not simply the result of his more active role. It obviously involved a change in Conrad's conception of his hero, and it marks a weakness in the book as a whole. It is apparent that the change in character depended upon a shift from A. P. Williams to some other source." Novelists had better adhere to their sources or else, and Sherry announces with satisfaction that because Conrad drops Source One and takes up Source Two, Jim breaks in half; the notion not having occurred to Sherry—as it would have to any novelist or reader—that Jim may be discontinuous, if he is, for a thousand other reasons, or seamless coming from a thousand sources. Scholarship isn't at its best sitting in the artist's chair acting out fantasies of creation.

Yet Conrad invites the wrong kind of attention. Reading *Nostromo*, for instance, one can't stop wondering how close to his authorities he is at any moment, what vignettes and histories are being scarcely disguised, what books the dispositions of his characters and the interiors of their old Spanish houses are being more or less painstakingly copied from. Sherry, having quoted a long passage from *Nostromo*, remarks that "Conrad has made use here of Eastwick's first impressions during his initial exploration of Valencia. . . . Eastwick's interpolations and forceful directives to his friend—'Now, mark me,' 'You see the large house on the right hand'—are very like Captain Mitchell's 'We enter now . . . ,' 'Observe the old Spanish houses,' and both men make use of white-covered umbrellas . . .": Sherry is absurd, but Conrad encourages him with the musty second-handness of the sham-impressionistic prose—

> Thus Captain Mitchell would talk in the middle of the Plaza, holding over his head a white umbrella with a green lining; but inside the cathedral, in the dim light, with a faint scent of incense floating in the cool atmosphere, and here and there a

kneeling female figure, black or all white, with a veiled head, his
lowered voice became solemn and impressive.

Conrad is a very bookish writer, though Henry James
(who plays here the maiden shyly palpating the Ancient Mari-
ner's stringy biceps and murmuring "Ah!") thought otherwise:
". . . [*The Mirror of the Sea*] is a wonder to me really—for
its so bringing home the prodigy of your past experiences:
bringing it home to me more personally and directly, I mean,
the immense treasure and the inexhaustible adventures. No one
has *known*—for intellectual use—the things you know. . . ."
Conrad himself was less persuaded of the immensity and inex-
haustibility, as Sherry demonstrates by quoting a recollection
of Edward Garnett's: "On one occasion, in describing to him a
terrible family tragedy of which I had been an eye-witness,
Conrad became visibly ill-humored and at last cried out with
exasperation, 'Nothing of the kind has ever come my way! I
have spent half my life knocking about in ships, only getting
ashore between voyages. I know nothing, nothing! except from
the outside. I have to guess at everything!' "
Conrad was exaggerating: the early novels weren't the
work of a writer who knew nothing. His personal knowledge of
men under stress, however, had dematerialized into literature
by the time he wrote *The Mirror of the Sea*; and James misad-
dressed to this plausible laureate exercise the enthusiasm he
might have conferred with some aptness on *The Nigger of the
"Narcissus"* or *Heart of Darkness* or *Typhoon*. As for *Nostromo, The Secret Agent*, and *Under Western Eyes*, they are
summer reading more or less entertainingly pieced together out
of hints and patches from what Conrad called "dull, wise
books," books of fact and reminiscence; the last novels are
worse, much shabbier; but, *Nostromo* and after, none of them
suggests a level of understanding usefully higher than that in
almost any of Conrad's magazine-stories—say, "Gaspar
Ruiz," in which Conrad is dispirited enough to write about "a
scoundrel of the deepest dye" and his "nefarious designs."
Conrad was an outsider from the beginning; his outburst
to Garnett was a genuine *cri de coeur*, he had to guess at everything; only, at the beginning he could sometimes make a virtue

of his exclusion: expatriate and exile, passing "half . . . [his] life knocking about in ships," never quite at home in the language he was in some of his early writing able to derive with desperate care from the strangeness of a nearly unintelligible world. Sherry's single success in his two ambitious books is his study of the sources of *Heart of Darkness*, the reasons being that for once his method doesn't get in the way of what Conrad is doing, and that what Conrad is doing is worth considering.

In *Heart of Darkness* Conrad transforms, particular by particular, with the most deliberate consistency of intention, the settled, built-up, commercially feasible, meanly purposeful quotidian Congo (of which his experience was so brief) into the prehistorically isolated and uninhabited, shelterless, impracticable, homicidally purposeless nightmare Congo of his desire. (Contemplating this process may lead the reader to regret the unhysterical novel that might have been made directly from the facts of the time and place, though Conrad himself wasn't the writer to have done it.) Throughout the novel Conrad suffers from the force of the outward and actual, which as far as possible he suppresses for the sake of an intensely simplified paradigm of his suffering. *Heart of Darkness* is sincere melodrama, whose agitation is disproportionate to its events but not to the author's unexaminable feelings. The duality of the novel is clear enough even in the relative straightforwardness of the opening pages, since despite Conrad's mode of presentation people do have names, things do have functions and purposes: "The business intrusted to this fellow," says Marlow, naming no names and finding no meanings, "was the making of bricks —so I had been informed; but there wasn't a fragment of a brick anywhere in the station, and he had been there more than a year—waiting"; yet, as Sherry points out with somewhat confounding solemnity, while Conrad was at Kinchassa the brickmaker there—"un spécialiste, M. De Ligne"—"far from . . . being idle, . . . seems to have been singularly active" making bricks. Or Marlow invents a graveyard of the approaching machine age—

> I came upon a boiler wallowing in the grass, then found a
> path leading up the hill. It turned aside for the boulders, and

also for an undersized railway-truck lying there on its back with its wheels in the air. One was off. The thing looked as dead as the carcass of some animal. I came upon more pieces of decaying machinery, a stack of rusty rails. To the left a clump of trees made a shady spot, where dark things seemed to stir feebly. I blinked, the path was steep. A horn tooted to the right, and I saw the black people run. A heavy and dull detonation shook the ground, a puff of smoke came out of the cliff, and that was all. No change appeared in the face of the rock. They were building a railway. The cliff was not in the way of anything; but this objectless blasting was all the work going on.

—a paragraph of Conradian theater which Sherry discredits by proving, with evidence from his sources, that building a railway takes a lot of work and makes a lot of noise, that railways are an efficient means of transportation, and that, since "the work on the railway was in its initial stages, and the first rails and sleepers had been brought out from Belgium on the vessel Conrad travelled in," it was doubtful Conrad would have had the "opportunity to observe a railway truck, machinery and rails . . . abandoned and rusting."

Sherry doesn't know that *Heart of Darkness* is unique among Conrad's novels, but his method gathers the evidence that permits us to follow the obsessively sustained procedure that makes it so. Conrad's procedure here is quite unlike his procedure not only in the later novels, for which customarily he transcribes from his reference-texts with alterations and additions as inert as the originals, but in such early novels as *The Nigger of the "Narcissus"* and *Typhoon* (neither of which Sherry discusses), for which he seems to have relied on a seaman's still scrupulously recollected personal and professional experiences that—what was impossible for him with the Congo voyage—he could bear to treat directly. "I am not," said Conrad, "a facile inventor. I have some imagination,—but that's another thing." *Heart of Darkness*, however, alone among his novels, is almost nothing except invention—a perverse sort of invention, consisting as it does mainly in distortion, omission, misrepresentation with the aim of denying the apparent and probable nature of the objects described. *Heart of Darkness* is Conrad's revenge for the Congo voyage he couldn't write about.

Photographs of Conrad are as they should be: the face is defensively bearded (not the unconcealing fringe of a horseshoe beard); the look is waxy and remote, as if its owner is already an exhibit at Madame Tussaud's. According to his wife, he was exceedingly nervous and anxiety-ridden, incapable of supporting the most insignificant bad news or disruption of routine if he were to go on writing or even staying alive from one day to the next (though, continuing to do his writing, he bore up for years under his unrelieved burden of financial anxiety with a fortitude that might have gratified many a wife). He was a man with a secret, but, since he was an intelligent and unpretentious man, the secret could have had nothing to do with the treasure-trove of inexhaustible riches that fulsome old taste-mongers like James impute to practitioners of the sacred craft. Conrad detested the job of writing, almost always did it with petrifying slowness, and as he grew older did it less and less well. He had also detested the sea, which he remembered as an occupation of stupefying boredom. He belonged nowhere. Sherry pauses for a moment, during his discussion of *Nostromo*, to characterize its author: "Father Corbelàn's condemnation of Decoud fits the creator of Decoud: 'You believe neither in stick nor stone.' " But not believing isn't not caring, and the secret may have had something to do with how, belonging nowhere and believing nothing, Conrad could care as painfully and unceasingly as he did.

IX.
Ellmann on Joyce, etc.

Carrying an inconspicuous sign that reads "I Am the Author of *James Joyce*," Richard Ellmann tells us as early as page 3 of this collection of essays[1] just why we don't like Boswell's *Life of Johnson* nearly as much as we think we do:

> More than anything else we want in modern biography to see the character forming, its peculiarities taking shape—but Boswell prefers to give it to us already formed. No doubt it was hard for Boswell to conceive of Dr. Johnson as a small boy in short trousers, at least until that short-trousered small boy began to translate Virgil and Homer. It is hard for us too. And primarily Boswell wants to reveal Johnson's *force* of character, while today we should ask him to disclose to us the inner compulsions, the schizoid elements—such is our modern vocabulary —which lay behind that force.

Boswell was shallow rather than deep, he couldn't ferret out and unflinchingly lay bare Johnson's *real* motives:

> A Boswell alive today would have difficulty in representing so amusingly Johnson's scorn for Scotsmen; he would feel the need to tell us the origins of this xenophobia, and much of the comedy would evaporate before cumbersome explanation. We should

---
[1]*Golden Codgers* (Oxford, 1974).

145

want to know more about Johnson's early indifference to religion, which began at the age of nine, he told Boswell, on account of his weak eyes—a curious explanation (was the prayer book badly printed?)—and continued until as a student at Oxford he happened upon William Law's *Serious Call to a Holy Life* and became religious again. This is the panoply of the mind, not its basic workings.

Sad, though, that Ellmann and the modern reader won't read Boswell a little more carefully, since they would learn that Johnson's explanation isn't at all curious or impenetrable: "I fell into an inattention to religion," he told Boswell, "or an indifference about it, in my ninth year. The church at Lichfield, in which we had a seat, wanted reparation, so I was to go and find a seat in other churches; and having bad eyes, and being awkward about this, I used to go and read in the fields on Sunday. This habit continued till my fourteenth year." In other words, the boy was so near-sighted that he balked at the prospect of stumbling over thresholds and outstretched legs in an unfamiliar church among strangers, listening to a sermon delivered by a stranger he couldn't see; so he went off to the fields with a book. As for Johnson's attitude toward Scotsmen, any biographer who "feel[s] the need to tell us the origin of this xenophobia" will probably also feel the need to dig up the Oedipal root of Shakespeare's attitude toward rural constables or a New Yorker's relish for jokes about hillbillies. Ellmann seems to think he's tackling, if not a Hitler, at least an Ezra Pound on the Rome radio; but some of Johnson's best friends were Scotsmen (including—maybe the modern reader doesn't know—Boswell), he made an extensive and friendly tour of Scotland, nor does he anywhere in his subsequent *Journey to the Western Islands of Scotland* advocate genocide or restrictive quotas. (His manservant for the last thirty-two years of his life was a Jamaican Negro freedman, Francis Barber, whom he treated as a son and a friend and eventually made the residuary legatee of his not inconsiderable estate.) Johnson was a very nice man and he was fond of many men, women, and children of every race and sex and he didn't practice cannibalism or discrimination.

He may, however, have practiced some sort of physical self-mortification, reluctantly abetted, at his desperate insistence, by Mrs. Thrale (the problematic evidence has been available for a long time; Katharine Balderston's essay, which Ellmann mentions as his source, takes a more humane and less thrilled view of it than Ellmann does). Boswell, says Ellmann (who doesn't seem to be familiar with Boswell's journals), would have filed and forgotten such "unseemly" stuff, whereas "Today we want to see our great men at their worst as well as their best." Indeed the modern biographer has scarcely begun; he takes for his motto "No worst, there is none"; and he looks lyrically forward to worse and worse:

> We can claim to be more intimate, but even our intimacy shows occasional restraints, little islands of guardedness in a blunt ocean [blunt oceans differ from sharp oceans, they are muddier and more obtuse and they belch up nasty little innuendoes, they are the pet oceans of modern biographers]. We have savoured [bold oral metaphor] the emotional convolutions of Lytton Strachey's love life with Carrington and their friends, but the precise anatomical convolutions [*la bête à deux dos*] remain shrouded [peel off the pall of the past!] by the last rags of biographical decorum [let it all hang out!]. . . .

There is a new breed of literary biographer. He aims at demonstrating that every writer's private life is as unseemly as ours; that nobody is any better than he has to be; that only the writer's "conscious direction . . . gives shape to what might otherwise be his run-of-the-mill phobias or obsessions and distinguishes his grand paranoia from our squirmy ones." Ellmann himself is dean of the squirmy biographers. The pioneer work is his biography of Joyce, published fifteen years ago; other examples since are Carlos Baker on Hemingway, Lawrance Thompson on Frost, Arthur Mizener on Ford Madox Ford.[2] A few quotations will illustrate the method.

On page 192 of *The Saddest Story*, having surveyed the

---

[2]Harry T. Moore's biography of Lawrence isn't quite in the same category: though its effect is similar, its hatred and condescension are unintentional. I discuss it in the chapter on Lawrence.

latest of Ford's accumulating personal troubles, Mizener remarks that "Ford was, as usual, broke." Ford was then thirty-five. He had already achieved a well-deserved position among the best-known men of letters of the age; he had written eleven novels; he had been Joseph Conrad's collaborator and friend; he had edited the best English literary review ever; he had been the discoverer, sponsor, and associate of the best of "*les jeunes*" (e.g., Pound, Lawrence, Wyndham Lewis); in his spare time he had had a nervous breakdown while leading an extremely complicated social and private life; he didn't gamble or make foolish investments; he worked very hard and hoped his books would sell and argued with publishers for better contracts; he was an excellent cook: but the tenured Ivy League professor, pausing for an occasional chat with his tax lawyer to maximize his profit from books about impecunious artists, is inexorable. Mozart was, as usual, broke.

The master of the method is Ellmann, who perfected it at once in his Joyce book with innumerable quick strokes of condescension and callous flippancy. Consider, for instance, the function of the epithet "lugubrious" and the phrase "with more friendliness than accuracy" in the following passage: "Joyce's activities on Sullivan's behalf were made more difficult by his fading eyesight. He had lugubrious discussions about this time with Aldous Huxley, also a victim of eye trouble, and with Thomas W. Pugh, a fellow-Dubliner who pleased him by knowing *Ulysses* and Dublin almost as intimately as he did himself. Pugh was blind in one eye, and Joyce eagerly asked his birth year, which was 1883; he then said with more friendliness than accuracy, 'We are much alike, both of us blind in one eye, and both born in the same year' " (but "we"—Ellmann, you, and I—remember that the year of Joyce's birth was 1882). Or Ellmann as dean of interior decorators: "He and Nora bought some furniture, undistinguished but comfortable." Lucia, Joyce's daughter, whom he loved dearly and spent years of his life and a great deal of his money taking from doctor to doctor throughout Europe in the hope of curing her mental illness, had just been carried off in a straitjacket to a sanitarium: "With Lucia at Ivry, Joyce had time for a new misfortune," chirps Ellmann; a few pages earlier he recorded a trip Joyce took "with the hapless Lucia in tow." Joyce's despair at his daughter's illness having overflowed in a heartbroken letter to Harriet Weaver, Ellmann comments that "Joyce had not wept in a letter since he suspected Nora of infidelity in 1909. Though not so blind as Homer, nor so exiled as Dante, he had reached his life's nadir." At such moments Ellmann may be said to have invented a new mode of swinishness. Lytton Strachey, who piqued himself on his malice, is all heart by comparison with these American professors and their corporate artillery of foundation grants, research assistants, unlimited access to letters and manuscripts, unlimited license to speak *ex cathedra* in huge and blackly footnoted tomes that say the official word on all the unfortunate geniuses of the twentieth century.

But Ellmann isn't content just to talk mean; now that censorship has collapsed he wants to talk both mean and dirty: such is the burden of *Golden Codgers*, and, fifteen years after *Joyce*, Ellmann shambles out for his last tango with the sniggering academic reader: "During seven years Gide and Wilde had five spurts of acquaintance," he commences the second paragraph of his essay on the Gide-Wilde relationship. On Pater the patron of sensuousness and Ruskin the puritan: "one was all infection and the other all contraception." On the prevalence of excremental images in Luther: "Psychohistorians will have to take account . . . of the possible banality of anality in Luther's time." On the phrase "boyish holiday" in Wilde's "*Hélas!*": "A 'boyish holiday' is . . . not the most offensive way to spend one's time, especially if one likes boys" (pederasty is Ellmann's most hilarious topic). So intent is Ellmann on exposing the butterfly's private parts that he actually conducts a lengthy critique of "*Hélas!*": regarding the terms Wilde applies to himself in the poem, Ellmann says that " 'ancient wisdom' and 'austere control'—self-congratulatory since Wilde never had either—are so vague as to constitute . . ." etc.; but the point is that *nobody*, not Epictetus or Spinoza, can apply such terms to himself, that the poem isn't so much silly or mendacious as non-existent and Ellmann is talking about nothing at all.

Now and then Ellmann's ill-will becomes in its indiscriminateness really alarming—maybe because it runs out of dirt and has to feed on thin air—as when it takes off after Arthur Symons:

> His interest in France was consolidated by a trip to Paris in 1889 with Havelock Ellis as his companion. They visited Mallarmé on one of his *mardis*, and met also Huysmans, Maeterlinck, and other prominent writers. Villiers, whom they had hoped to see, disobliged them by dying shortly before their arrival, but Symons wrote an obituary article on him for Oscar Wilde's *Woman's World* in the same year.

Whom or what does Ellmann think he is mocking? Symons's triviality in making a journey to meet prominent writers? in being accompanied by—har! har! har!—Havelock Ellis? in hoping to see Villiers? in not anticipating Villiers's death? in presuming he could make up for not meeting Villiers by writing an obituary piece about him? and publishing it in a magazine with such a ridiculous name edited by so trivial a writer? Is it Villiers's absurd disobligingness in dying a few days too early? What on earth *amuses* Ellmann here? And the only rational answer seems to be that Ellmann has already decided, dipping his poisoned darts, that just about the whole population out there are trivial and ridiculous whatever they do: "good sport it is to see a man tumble with an epilepsy, and revive and tumble again, and all this he knows not why." Two centuries ago somebody named Soame Jenyns published a moral treatise which explained that human suffering was justified because it furnished occupation and amusement, somewhere high up along the great stair of creation, for a species of beings superior to man; and Samuel Johnson,[3] reviewing the treatise, took the opportunity to imagine this species at work and play: "Many a merry bout have these frolic beings at the vicissitudes of an ague, and good sport it is to see a man tumble with an epilepsy, and revive and tumble again, and all this he knows not why." There is no substitute for fellow-feeling. Ellmann, ambitious to do the twentieth century, ends by doing it in. Tone is the man. Unluckily Ellmann's tone, which is the pride and courage that drives him to perform his impressive labors,

---

[2]Whose attitude toward people (as I tried to show in Chapter IV) was about as different as possible from Ellmann's.

disfigures whatever it touches; and he doesn't understand that tone is everything.

Surprisingly, discussing Eliot and Pound in the final essay of *Golden Codgers*, Ellmann chickens out and is altogether respectful, he even writes pretty well. The essay considers the first draft of *The Waste Land*, and pays the proper tribute to Pound by documenting his indispensable services to the poem. Surely, for instance, if Pound's advice to delete such lines as these had not been followed—

> Fresca slips softly to the needful stool,
> Where the pathetic tale of Richardson
> Eases her labour till the deed is done. . . .
> This ended, to the steaming bath she moves,
> Her tresses fanned by little flutt'ring Loves;
> Odours, confected by the cunning French,
> Disguise the good old hearty female stench . . .

—if Eliot had held out for such neo-Swiftian hysteria (erupting through the pseudo-Popean façade), the poem could hardly have imposed itself as the credo of a generation; and it might well have appeared to be what Eliot himself irritably called it a generation later: "a personal and wholly insignificant grouse against life." And of course against women. The first draft of *The Waste Land* testifies stunningly—and recalls the less obvious evidence of the other poems—that Eliot's reputation for representativeness depends on what was *omitted* from his poems. (If he had put it all back and said it in his own unaltered voice, his poems might even have shocked a few readers and would in any case never have passed as good gray poems bequeathed to us, along with some incidental unpleasantnesses, by the Nobel Laureate.) Ellmann is interested enough in the Eliot-Pound collusion to keep his eye on the object and a civil tongue in his head; the essay is a responsible one. As Ellmann might sum it up: Though neither panoply nor basic workings, it's Ellmann's book's comfortable if undistinguished little zenith, without more than a spurt or two of his squirmy impudence.

X.

Chekhov

Not yet out of his twenties Chekhov already had a celebrity second only to Tolstoy's among Russian writers of the time; but he never set up as a great man. He was a *Wunderkind* unspoiled by success, a brilliant and unpretentious personality, a boyish charmer who charmed Tolstoy himself to tears. Great writer and great personality; yet the personality doesn't coincide—as in Tolstoy or Dostoevsky it entirely does—with the writer. Of course Tolstoy knew both: from the first recognized and admired Chekhov the "true poet and artist" of the stories; also knew well face to face the "simply wonderful" Chekhov, "the dear, beautiful man," the irresistible presence whose lack of affectation, quickness of wit, irreverence, candor, clarity, guile, panache, and uncapturability survive, for us, not so much in Chekhov's formal *oeuvre* as in his letters.[1] We are delighted, for example, by the correspondent who, writing home from his journey across Siberia, brings up for comparison these nuances of Siberian and Russian etiquette: "On entering a Siberian bedroom at night you are not assailed by the peculiar Russian stench. True, handing me a teaspoon, an old woman wiped it

---

[1] Avrahm Yarmolinsky (ed.), *Letters of Anton Chekhov* (New York, 1973); Simon Karlinsky (ed.), *Letters of Anton Chekhov* (New York, 1973).

on her behind, but then they will not serve you tea without a tablecloth, people don't belch in your presence, don't search for insects in their hair . . ."; or, staying at a farm on the Don Steppe with the neolithic family he later memorialized in his story "The Pecheneg," describes their strenuous way of life:

> Latrines, ashtrays, and other amenities are unknown, unless you travel for some half a dozen miles. To relieve yourself (irrespective of the weather), you have to walk down into the ravine and choose a bush; you are warned not to sit down until you have convinced yourself that under the bush there is no troublesome rattlesnake or some other creature.
>
> The population: old man Kravtzov and his wife, also Pyotr, a Cossack cornet, and several other children, as well as Nikita, a shepherd, and Akulina, a cook. Of dogs there is no end, and they are all ferocious, allowing no one to pass, day or night. I need a constant escort, or else the number of Russia's men of letters will diminish by one. The worst creature is Mukhtar, an old hound from whose mug dirty tow is suspended instead of hair. He hates me and every time I leave the house he rushes at me with a savage roar. . . .
>
> The main occupation is rational agronomy, which was introduced by the young cornet, who acquired 5 rubles' and 40 copecks' worth of books on agriculture. The main branch of the economy is ceaseless day-long killing. They kill sparrows, swallows, bumblebees, magpies, ravens so that they should not eat the bees; they kill bees so that they should not damage the blossoms of the fruit trees, and fell trees so that they should not impoverish the soil. The result is a peculiar cycle based on the latest scientific data.
>
> We go to bed at nine. Sleep is disturbed by the howls of the dogs in the courtyard, and under my couch another hound barks fiercely in response to them. A discharge of firearms wakes me up: through the window my hosts fire rifles at some animal that is damaging the economy. To leave the house at night it is necessary to wake up the cornet, or else the dogs will tear you to pieces. The result is that the cornet's sleep depends on the quantity of tea and milk that I had drunk previously.

Years later, however, Chekhov expanded and disintegrated this material into the pathos of "The Pecheneg," which attempts an introspective representation of the old Cossack's fear of death (with tactless echoes of Tolstoy's Ivan Ilych: "And now he kept thinking and he longed to pitch upon some significant thought unlike others, which would be a guide to him in life, and he wanted to think out principles of some sort for himself so as to make his life as deep and earnest as he imagined himself to be").

Chekhovian pathos is sometimes an attempt to ventilate or refine opaque, refractory, unliterary material. Always the theoretical spokesman for objectivity as the whole of the writer's art, Chekhov in his own stories isn't above forcing a Cossack farmer or a Moscow merchant to carry on like Hamlet. But in his letters, taking for granted as well as expressly stating that "the heart of another is a darkness," he seems content to exercise introspection only on himself and let God take care of old man Kravtzov; trusts appearances and gives his mettlesome comic improvisation plenty of room:

> Very well—I'll get married, if that's what you want. But my conditions are: everything will have to be as it was before—that is, she'll have to live in Moscow, while I'll live in the country and make trips to see her. As for the sort of bliss that persists day in and day out, from one morning to the next—I won't be able to take it. When I'm told day after day about the same thing in the same tone of voice, I become ferocious. I become ferocious in the company of Sergeyenko, for instance, because he looks very much like a woman ("intelligent and responsive") and because when I'm with him the notion pops into my head that my wife may possibly look like him. I promise to be a splendid husband, but give me the sort of wife who, like the moon, won't appear in my heaven every night. I won't write any better just because I get married.

This little comedy of temperament was dashed off by Chekhov at thirty-five, parrying the usual advice from one's married best friend. By an irony of fate—it could have been a Chekhov story —Chekhov eventually got just what he told Alexey Suvorin he wanted: a wife (the actress Olga Knipper) who lived and worked in Moscow while Chekhov for his failing health had to languish in the provinces; and at forty, very ill with tuberculosis, Chekhov responds to a typical joke from one's betrothed (Olga had heard, so she wrote, that he was giving her up for a priest's daughter) by turning it into a cameo of a bedroom farce:

> Thank you for your good wishes on the occasion of my marriage. I informed my fiancée of your intention of coming to Yalta in order to make trouble for her. She replied that she would not let me out of her embraces when that "wicked woman" came to Yalta. I observed that to remain in someone's embraces for so long in hot weather was unhygienic. She took offense and became thoughtful, as if trying to guess in what circle I had learned that *façon de parler*, and after a short while she announced that the theater is evil and that my decision to write no more plays was in every way laudatory, and asked me to kiss her. To this I answered that now, since I have the rank of an Academician, it did not behoove me to kiss frequently. She burst into tears, and I left.

"Do write, or there will be trouble," he archly ends one letter to Suvorin; and ends another with a postscript: "Wire me about something. I love to receive telegrams." Their friendship is as puzzling to us as many friendships are from the outside, especially one so far in the past and with so little surviving evidence. Suvorin was the elder by twenty-six years, a minor literary figure who by the time Chekhov knew him had become the wealthy publisher of a crudely reactionary St. Petersburg newspaper. During the Dreyfus case, while Chekhov, in Nice for his health, was writing Suvorin careful, lucid, incontestable accounts ("I know the case from the stenographic report") of Dreyfus's innocence and Zola's heroism, *New Times* kept thundering away at an international Jewish "Syndicate" that was suborning even so-called impartial observers with huge bribes: in a dry parenthesis to Suvorin, Chekhov takes note of the imputation by confessing that he has already been bought with "a hundred francs from the Jews." Suvorin had been an early and influential literary patron of Chekhov's, and gratitude no doubt played a part in Chekhov's feeling for him; Chekhov's father, a dull and violent man, had terrorized his wife and children, and Chekhov ("There was no childhood in my childhood") may in compensation have welcomed acquaintance with an older man as shrewd and worldly as Suvorin. Or one can give up and merely summarize: because Chekhov was a man of unfailing civic conscience and Suvorin a conscious, unscrupulous, energetic flunky of autocratic repression, the two of them had many disagreements; but they enjoyed each other's company wherever they could have it, traveled together as often as convenience permitted, and talked on into the night whenever they met. "I'm passionately eager to have a talk with you," writes Chekhov, back from his six-months' voyage to Sakhalin, and moved to offer a declaration of personal commitment unique in his correspondence: "I'm seething inside. You're the only one I want because you're the only one I can talk to." Chekhov's friendship with Suvorin was the closest and most enduring of his life; his only intimacy.

Another relationship of Chekhov's that puzzles us here and now was his long flirtation with a friend of his sister's, Lydia Mizinova: "Lika." Yarmolinsky's edition of the letters, which is a good general sampling, includes thirteen to Lika; whereas Karlinsky, setting out to "put together a coherent intellectual portrait," omits "the flirtatious letters to various women [Lika explicitly] who were of no real importance in his life." Women may wish to debate with Professor Karlinsky the question: Are a man's flirtations merely necessary but otherwise insignificant, like stops at the service station or the barber's? even flirtations he sustains for ten years? even one with a woman as desperately in love with Chekhov as Lika was, whom his letters smother with a coy and impenetrable charade of gallantry ("Bewitching, astounding Lika! . . . Yours from head to heels, with all my soul and all my heart, until my tombstone, to the point of self-oblivion, of stupefaction, of frenzy"[2])? But don't applaud Yarmolinsky yet, since for some reason he includes none of the letters—to Lika or

---

[2] As well as less courtly phrases in a letter he fabricated and sent to Lika for her inspection; it was addressed to "Trofim," the lover he had invented for her: "Trofim! You son of a bitch. If you don't stop pursuing Lika, I'll shove a corkscrew into you, you cheap riffraff, in the place that rhymes with lass. Ah, you turd! . . ." Neither K. nor Y. prints this letter. It is quoted in Ernest J. Simmons, *Chekhov* (Boston, 1962), p. 287.

anybody else—from Chekhov's travels with Suvorin in Western Europe during the fall of 1894.

Lika is in Switzerland at the time, involved, as Chekhov knows, in a liaison with a friend of his, Potapenko; and Chekhov keeps trying to track her down: "Potapenko told me that you would be in Switzerland. If this is so, write me exactly where in Switzerland so I can look you up. Of course, I'd be delighted to see you." When at last he hears from her, he gets the news—"What was there for me to do, Daddy? You always managed to escape and shove me off on someone else"—that Lika is pregnant and Potapenko has absconded; all she wants now is to see Chekhov and talk with him: "I don't think you would cast a stone at me. It seems to me that you were always indifferent to people, to their inadequacies and weaknesses." Chekhov thereupon writes his sister at once that he has wearied of traveling and will come home early: "I had counted on seeing Lika in Paris, but it now develops that she is in Switzerland." To Lika he writes (no more charades): "Unfortunately, I cannot go to Switzerland, for I'm with Suvorin [he had been with Suvorin all the time, for instance when he wrote Lika that he would be delighted to see her in Switzerland]"; and there is a single ominous sentence of offended dignity: "You ought not to have written about my indifference to people." The episode[3] doesn't interest editors who would rather settle for a grand or poignant portrait, but it's a fascinating wart nevertheless.

Chekhov wasn't a prude, quite the contrary. Within a year he had used the Lika-Potapenko affair sympathetically (indeed sentimentally) in *The Sea Gull.* Nor did he categorically reject, except from a woman who was presuming to make something momentous out of a flirtation, the charge of indifference: on another occasion, writing to Suvorin, he maintained that "in this world it is necessary to be indifferent. Only indifferent peo-

---

[3]This summary of it is taken from Simmons, pp. 324-327. "Verochka," a story Chekhov wrote several years before he met "the beautiful Lika," concerns a girl passionately in love with a man "affected . . . by the insuperable habit of looking at things objectively, which often hinders people from living."

ple can see things clearly, be fair, and work—that, of course, applies only to people who are honorable and intelligent; egoists and brainless people are indifferent as it is." What is indifference? Chekhov certainly wasn't indifferent, in the customary sense, to women: over many years in many places he was a very active ladies' man. (For those who have read Chekhov only in the standard selections that emphasize his pathos, gentleness, forbearance—at worst, his disenchantment—one of the surprises of the relatively comprehensive Constance Garnett edition is to discover how many Maupassant-like cynical and knowing stories of bourgeois adultery he bothered to write.) "To take revenge on the censors [who had cut up a story of his on the perils of marriage] and all those who gloated over my misfortune, my friends and I are forming a Cuckolding Society. The constitution has already been submitted for approval. I was elected chairman by a majority of fourteen to three." He had every qualification for the office: tall, handsome, young, famous, vivacious, gallant, not given to telling all; electrically alert to amorous opportunities wherever he happened to be, as, on his way home from Sakhalin, during a brief stopover in Ceylon ("When I have children, I'll say to them, not without pride: 'Why, you sons of bitches, I've had relations in my day with a black-eyed Hindu girl, and guess where? In a coconut grove, on a moonlit night!' "); or in the two metropolises, where it might have taken Leporello and a new catalogue aria to do him justice (back at his country estate after a visit to Moscow, he told Suvorin that "girls, girls, girls" had been among his chief occupations while he was there; his conquests in Moscow and St. Petersburg were legendary if not mythical).

"I have very little passion," Chekhov said in response to a comment on his writing. He had no memories of affection: "When I was a child, I was so rarely caressed that even now, as an adult, I react to caresses as something unheard of, unknown." At sixteen he was living alone in his native Taganrog supporting himself as a tutor, and sending money to Moscow where his father, mother, brothers, and sister had moved after the failure of his father's grocery; from the age of nineteen, he supported his family with income from his writing while he managed to complete his studies at the medical school and became a practicing physician. "His unceasing solicitude for his family, his kindness to his friends, should not give rise to illusions. Unquestionably he was doing—and would continue to do—a great deal for them, but it was not because of surges of affection; there is no cry from the heart in his letters to his brothers, for instance, or in his notes to Leikin, his most regular correspondent during this period. His charity was conscious, his spirit of devotion was deliberate. . . ."[4]

By his early twenties symptoms of tuberculosis were already evident. He had a chronically very painful and incapacitating case of hemorrhoids, which he attributed not only to his "sedentary life" but to "my excesses *in Baccho et Veneris*" (besides the ladies, he liked all-night parties and heavy drinking, and he hated to be alone). "The constant nervous strain under which he lived, aggravated by overwork and money worries, soon made itself felt. [His brother] Michael records that 'the moment he fell asleep, he began "to jerk." He would suddenly wake up terrified, a strange force seemed to throw him up on the bed, something inside him seemed to be torn up "by the root," he would jump out of bed and could not go to sleep for a long time.' "[5] By the age of twenty-seven he had written six hundred short stories. "What aristocratic writers take from nature gratis," he wrote to Suvorin at twenty-nine,

> the less privileged must pay for with their youth. Try and write a story about a young man—the son of a serf, a former grocer, choirboy, schoolboy and university student, raised on respect for rank, kissing the priests' hands, worshiping the ideas of others, and giving thanks for every piece of bread, receiving frequent whippings, making the rounds as a tutor without galoshes, brawling, torturing animals, enjoying dinners at the houses of rich relatives, needlessly hypocritical before God and man merely to acknowledge his own insignificance—write about how this young man squeezes the slave out of himself drop by drop and how, on waking up one fine morning, he finds that the

---

[4]Daniel Gillès, *Chekhov: Observer Without Illusion* (New York, 1968), p. 60.
[5]David Magarshack, *Chekhov* (Westport, 1970), p. 72.

blood coursing through his veins is no longer the blood of a
slave, but that of a real human being.

Chekhov never himself wrote such a story, especially with so
unlikely an ending. "My soul has wasted away," he wrote
Suvorin in a bleaker mood, "because of the awareness that I
am working for the sake of money and that money is the center
of my activity. This nagging feeling, together with the justice of
it, makes my writing a contemptible occupation in my eyes, I
have no respect for what I write, I am listless and bore my own
self, and I am glad I have medicine which, no matter what, I
am following not for the sake of money, after all."

At thirty, to the dismay of his family and friends, he went
off on his self-imposed journey of six thousand miles to investigate the penal colonies of Sakhalin, and was away from Russia for six months. The literary result was the strangest piece
he ever wrote, his only book-length work, *The Island of Sakhalin*: half of it unassimilated information and statistics, one
quarter indignant predictable sociology (conditions are so bad
that no rehabilitation is possible and all the convicts, even
those free to live in the villages, are hopelessly dehumanized),
one quarter diamond-hard bits of Chekhovian observation (sly,
brisk, opinionated convicts telling their stories to the visitor
and leading quite bearable lives as if neither they nor Chekhov
had ever heard of the doctrinaire sociology on the next or
previous page). The journey made him feel that he had *done*
something, and it was only at the moment of his return from
Sakhalin that he could describe himself as "passionately
eager" for something; in the instance, for a talk with Suvorin;
but it was an impulse that never got mentioned again in his
correspondence. At thirty-seven, sitting in a Moscow restau-
rant with Suvorin, he had his first massive tubercular hemorrhage.

He wanted to give, or give away, whatever he had. He was
endlessly generous with his time, his public wisdom, his professional skills, his money (though money was a perpetual anxiety, and he never seemed to have enough for himself and his
family). He spent a great deal of time reading, annotating,

editing, even rewriting unsolicited manuscripts from young writers:

> A promising author might be urged to send him still more stories to read. Or he would try to place the manuscripts himself or personally talk to a publisher in an effort to interest him in putting out a book for a beginner. . . . If one could not give everything that was asked, he insisted, one must at least give something. In responding to requests for help, he never worried about being deceived by imposters. It was better to be deceived by them, he argued, then fail to answer an appeal for assistance.[6]

His political attitudes were models of intelligence, humaneness, and practicality, in the shadow of a bigoted, sanctimonious, repressive government (quite like his father) that, luckily, wasn't efficient enough to be totalitarian: when Gorky's membership in the Academy was canceled for political reasons, Chekhov resigned with a letter of protest; when scholarly young Jews were recommended to him, he pulled strings to try to get them past the racial laws into the schools; with money he collected (some of it from Suvorin), he built local schools for the peasants; his book on Sakhalin had its intended effect of instigating reforms in the penal system; on every public issue that came up in his letters—not only his letters to the publisher and perpetrator of shameless government-dictated slanders, Suvorin—he presented transparently, at length, and with unanswerable exactness the argument of common decency:

> Your [Suvorin's] columns on the disturbances were unsatisfactory, and could not be otherwise, because no one can pass judgment in print on the disturbances when all mention of the facts is prohibited. The state forbade you to write, it forbids the truth to be told, that is arbitrary rule, and you talk lightheartedly about the rights and prerogatives of the state in connection with this arbitrary rule. The mind refuses to accept this combination as logical. You talk about the rights of the state, but you're disregarding what is legal. Rights and justice are the same for the state as for any juridical person. If the state wrongfully

---

[6]Simmons, pp. 115-116.

alienates a piece of my land, I can bring an action against it and the court will re-establish my right to that land. Shouldn't the same rules apply when the state beats me with a riding crop? Shouldn't I raise a hue and cry over my violated rights if it commits violence upon me? The concept of the state should be founded on definite legal relationships. If it is not, it is a bogey-man, an empty sound that produces an imaginary fright.[7]

During the famine of 1891 he collected relief funds and tried against calculated governmental obstruction to organize large-scale relief projects: the peasants were selling their horses to buy food, and Chekhov helped develop a plan to buy up the horses in order to keep them alive through the winter and turn them back to the peasants the following spring. At Melikhovo, the country estate where he lived for six years, he carried on without remuneration a very busy medical practice among the neighboring peasants and kept a pharmacy for them at his own expense. He spent months assisting in a census of his district (he had already, while in Sakhalin, done the first census there: ten thousand filled-out cards summing up interviews all of which, so far as is known, were conducted and transcribed by Chekhov himself). When a cholera epidemic threatened, he volunteered his services to the local authorities, begging money and hospital space from gentry, monks, factory-owners; he wrote to Suvorin that in a few weeks he had treated a thousand patients:

> My soul is weary. I'm bored. Not to belong to oneself, to think only of diarrhea, to start up at night from the dog's barking and a knock at the gate (haven't they come for me?), to drive jades along unknown roads, to read about and expect nothing but cholera, and at the same time to be entirely indifferent to this

---

[7]At the other end of the political spectrum, among the radicals, he found equally cogent evidence for his astonishing prophecy regarding post-Tsarist Russia: "Under the banner of science, art, and a protest against the suppression of free thought, among us in Russia there will reign toads and crocodiles of a sort that even Spain did not know at the time of the Inquisition. Well, you will see it! Narrowmindedness, great pretensions, inordinate self-love, and complete absence of a literary and social conscience will do their work. . . ."

illness and the people you serve—that, my dear sir, is a mess
that might do in anyone.

The "mess" could certainly be discounted here as a simple
enough temporary consequence of terrible and heroic strain
and fatigue; but it was a state of mind very common in Chekhov even when he was comparatively inactive and unharassed.
His code-word for it was "boredom," a word that for twenty
years was "a kind of leitmotif in his correspondence"[8]: "I'm
bored, although from a detached point of view cholera has its
interesting sides"; "depressing boredom"; "enormously
bored"; "No signs of boredom so far"; "For all that, I am
bored"; "Days of greatest boredom"; I am so terribly bored";
"For the time being things aren't too boring"; "I'm bored, but
not in the *Wellschmerz* sense"; "Is it growing old [he wrote at
thirty-two] or just boredom with living? I don't know, but I
have no very great desire to live. Or to die, either; but really I
have had about enough of living"; (inviting a friend to visit him
in Yalta) "Tolstoy is here and Gorky is here, so you won't be
bored, I hope"; so often in his letters to his wife that at last she
struck back, alarmed, "You're always bored!"; so often to
Gorky that the customarily quite respectful younger man ventured to rebuke him—"it's very unpleasant to read in your letters that you are bored. It is utterly unbecoming to you, you
see, and entirely unnecessary." Chekhov's usual way of dealing
with it was to go off on a trip somewhere, St. Petersburg or Sakhalin or Paris, but it stuck to him like a label (barely off the
train in Nice: "I'm already cruelly bored here"). The "mess"
he describes to Suvorin is a kind of terminal boredom; what he
himself calls—but wouldn't let Lika call—his "indifference to
people": the failure of sympathy, the breakdown of connection
(idle curiosity, random sensual impulse, fellow-feeling, loving-
kindness, charity, domestic affection) that not uncommonly
afflicts men in their forties as (in Eric Hoffer's image) the glow
of sensuality begins to fade. Tolstoy experienced it at fifty and
described it in "A Confession": suffering something like a paralysis of the will and just managing to restrain himself from

suicide, he eventually came out of it as a self-made religious ideologue with new (fewer and more inflexible) lines of connection that would protect him from it for the rest of his life. Chekhov's experience of it was in many ways special; more subtle and more debilitating. It seems to have been a familiar condition of his consciousness almost from boyhood, and (therefore?) never occurred as a crisis with flashes of panic and temptations to suicide; it was compatible with, indeed seemed to provoke, prodigies of physical, mental, and even erotic activity; it didn't inhibit his will and intelligence, which continued to operate as if they had all the accustomed sanctions of impulse and feeling; it made its appearance as a tone, a kind of darkening.

Tolstoy's only reservation after their first meeting was that the charming young man (with whom Tolstoy's daughter Tatyana fell in love at first sight!) "seems not to have a definite point of view"; on a later occasion he remarked that Chekhov wasn't "religious": misgivings that may have taken the names of Tolstoy's new ideology but were nonetheless attentive to a quality in Chekhov. Tolstoy, perhaps because of the delicacy of his feelings toward Chekhov, said nothing to him on the matter; but others, who had similar misgivings, spoke out. Suvorin, for instance, having read "The Horse-Stealers," asserted that it had no moral basis or point of view (no belief, no "religion"), that it was so "objective" as to shirk its moral responsibility; and Chekhov replied with one of his capsule manifestoes:

> You upbraid me about objectivity, styling it indifference to good and evil, absence of ideals and ideas, etc. You would have me say, in depicting horse thieves, that stealing horses is an evil. But then, that has been known a long while, even without me. Let jurors judge then, for my business is only to show them as they are. I write: You are dealing with horse thieves—know, then, that these are no beggars but men with full bellies, that these men belong to a cult, and that stealing horses is not simply stealing but a passion. Of course, it would be gratifying to couple art with sermonizing, but, personally, I find this exceedingly difficult and, because of conditions imposed by technique, all but impossible. Why, in order to depict horse thieves in seven hundred lines I must constantly think and speak as they

do and feel in keeping with their spirit; otherwise, if I add a pinch of subjectivity, the images will become diffused and the story will not be as compact as it behooves all short stories to be. When I write, I rely fully on the reader, on the assumption that he himself will add the subjective elements that are lacking in the story. . . .

Doubtless it's the tendency in Chekhov's early pieces—among them such superb comic sketches as "Frost," "The Pipe," "The Malefactor," "Sergeant Prishibeyev"—for the whole job to be done by observation, dramatization, an economy of quick external strokes; certainly it's the mode of which Chekhov at his characteristic best is the supreme master, it evolves into the lean unmoralized vividness of such mature masterpieces as "Gusev" and "The Murder." Still, once Chekhov graduated from skits and squibs, he often introduced elements into his fiction that "coupled art with sermonizing," that added a pound as well as a pinch of subjectivity. Both he and Suvorin, intent on disagreeing, fail to notice the incorrectness of their mutual assumption: that Chekhov's fiction is invariably objective. Now in fact "The Horse-Stealers" is mostly as objective as Chekhov and Suvorin think it altogether is: a crisp, vigorous, dispassionate account of "an empty-headed fellow" who gets cheated and robbed of horse and gear by a pair of horse-thieves and their accomplice, the tavern-keeper's daughter. Only, the story has a very odd, apparently unironic coda, in which the protagonist keeps rehearsing and embroidering the lesson he has learned: "Who says it's a sin to enjoy oneself? . . . Those who have never lived in freedom like Merik and Kalashnikov, and have never loved Lyubka; they have been beggars all their lives, have lived without any pleasure, and have only loved their wives, who are like frogs"; and he goes on to the end finding moral and metaphysical reasons for cheating and stealing. The coda is a kind of inadvertent palinode: no empty-headed fellow is likely to be so ambitiously rational; and his implausible reflections expose, not the impact of experience on a simpleton, but Chekhov's own envious admiration of the amoral energy which in the story proper he has been content to observe and dramatize. So in his manifesto Chekhov is doubly wrong, and for the wrong reasons Suvorin's criticism of "The Horse-Stealers" is justified, because the total effect of this finally most unobjective story is to attack traditional morality ("belief") without suggesting an alternative that reads better than an adolescent's daydream.

Critics who wish to prove that Chekhov doesn't lack belief have several texts of his in evidence: "My holy of holies is the human body, health, intelligence, talent, inspiration, love and the most absolute freedom imaginable"; "there is greater love for man in electricity and steam than in continence and abstention from meat"; "God's world is good. Only one thing isn't good: ourselves." The sentiments are unexceptionable (except for the slight flavor of smugness in the last), but they resemble the sentiments of a critic (one of Suvorin's hacks on *New Times*) who, disliking Chekhov's cheerlessness, proclaimed that "The greatest miracle is man himself" and "The aim of life is life itself"; whereupon Chekhov retorted, "This isn't life, it's caramels." Chekhov has beliefs (some of them caramels) but no belief. The tone of his stories, when he loses confidence in their *ad hoc* moral configurations, their objectivity, wavers between the pyrrhonism of "The Horse-Stealers"[9] and the hollow pathos of "The Pecheneg."

The tone of his plays too. Consider these caramels, out of the mouths of characters toward whom the author shows every sign of approval:

> . . . what matters is not fame, not glory, not what I used to dream about, it's how to endure, to bear my cross, and have faith. I have faith and it all doesn't hurt me so much, and when I think of my calling I'm not afraid of life.

* * *

> . . . when I pass the peasants' woods that I have saved from being chopped down, or when I hear the sound of my young wood rustling, the stand I planted with my own hands, I realize that climate too is a little in my power, and that a thousand

---

[9]"Ward No. 6" has as its ostensible theme: One must care! But the tone of the story demonstrates the impossibility of caring about anything except the avoidance of pain, and pain won't do as a synecdoche of reality. Chekhov's characters are too small for his universe.

years from now if man should be happy, why, then I'll be a small part of that too. . . .

* * *

How shall I put it? It seems to me that everything on earth must change little by little and is already changing before our very eyes. In two or three hundred, eventually a thousand, years— it's not a matter of time—a new, happy life will come. We won't share in that life, of course, but we are living for it now, working, well—suffering; we are creating it—and in that alone lies the purpose of our being and, if you like, our happiness.

—on all of which (from *The Sea Gull, Uncle Vanya,* and *The Three Sisters,* respectively) there is a handy comment: "The greatest miracle is man himself." Partisans of Chekhov's drama will be glad to explain the type-casting and repetitiveness of the plays—moony girls, suicidal young men, philosophical tippling doctors, *fin-de-siècle* freeze-frame tableaux, disquisitions on the need for work, work, work and on the promise of life a thousand years from now—nor are they abashed by the bursts of gunfire in all but the last of the five full-length plays (Ivanov's suicide, Treplev's two attempts of which only the second is successful, Uncle Vanya's attempt to murder Serebryakov, Tusenbach's death in a duel). But Chekhov's own afterthoughts in *The Cherry Orchard* are more to the point: Epihodov's revolver ("I read all kinds of remarkable books, but the trouble is I cannot discover my own inclinations, whether to live or to shoot myself, but nevertheless, I always carry a revolver on me"); the moony housemaid, Dunyasha ("Like a flower—I am such a sensitive girl, I love tender words awfully"); Gayev, whom everybody tells to shut up when he is about to launch a philosophical disquisition. *The Cherry Orchard*, not only a witty parody of the earlier plays, has a vertebrate plot, distinct and credibly motivated characters, and an earned pathos: "Oh, my childhood, my innocence!" exclaims Lyubov Andreyevna, looking from the window of her old nursery out to the orchard, and reminding us of the very different life in Paris she has left behind and will soon be going back to.

The Cherry Orchard is an attractive and resourceful comedy; but Chekhov's element is fiction. In fiction the stance of objectivity that is so important to his idea of himself has a

responsible rôle *inside* the medium (Chekhov the dramatist
seems to assume that, because drama is by definition "objective" and the dramatist isn't *in* the play at all, he can allow his
characters to talk like sentimental novelists without himself in-
curring any responsibility for what they say). Much of the
strength of the great novella "Peasants" is in the unengaged
steadiness of the presentation, which establishes without pathos
or didacticism the range of these ordinary lives, and unempha-
tically accommodates the most extraordinary moment in Chekhov's fiction—while the family sleeps, the return of Fyokla
(Helen and Odysseus at once) from her nocturnal wanderings:

> "Oh, Lord!" sighed the cook.
> Someone rapped gently, ever so gently, at the window. It
> must have been Fyokla, come back. Olga got up, and yawning
> and whispering a prayer, unlocked the door, then pulled the bolt
> of the outer door. But no one came in; only there was a cold
> draft of air from the street and the entry suddenly grew bright
> with moonlight. Through the open door could be seen the silent,
> deserted street, and the moon itself floating across the sky.
> "Who's there?" called Olga.
> "Me," came the answer, "it's me."
> Near the door, hugging the wall, stood Fyokla, stark
> naked. She was shivering with cold, her teeth were chattering,
> and in the bright moonlight she looked very pale, strange, and
> beautiful. The shadows and the bright spots of moonlight on her
> skin stood out sharply, and her dark eyebrows and firm, young
> breasts were defined with peculiar distinctness.
> "The ruffians over there stripped me and turned me out
> like this," she muttered. "I had to go home without my clothes
> —mother-naked. Bring me something to put on."
> "But come inside," Olga said softly, beginning to shiver
> too.
> "I don't want the old folks to see." Granny was, in fact, al-
> ready stirring and grumbling, and the old man asked: "Who's
> there?" Olga brought out her own shift and skirt, dressed Fyok-
> la, and then both went softly into the house, trying to close the
> door noiselessly.
> "Is that you, you slick one?" Granny grumbled angrily,
> guessing who it was. "Curse you, you nightwalker! Why don't
> the devil take you!"

"It's all right, it's all right," whispered Olga, wrapping Fyokla up; "it's all right, dearie."

All was quiet again. They always slept badly; each one was kept awake by something nagging and persistent: the old man by the pain in his back, Granny by anxiety and malice, Marya by fear, the children by itch and hunger. Now, too, their sleep was restless; they kept turning from one side to the other, they talked in their sleep, they got up for a drink.

Fyokla suddenly burst out into a loud, coarse howl, but checked herself at once, and only sobbed from time to time, her sobs growing softer and more muffled until she was still. Occasionally from the other side of the river came the sound of the striking of the hours; but the clock struck oddly—first five and then three.

"Oh, Lord!" sighed the cook.

"Peasants" is Chekhov's fulfillment as the honest and unerring, the objective, writer he wished to be; master of surface and routine, of the radiance of ordinariness. ("In the Ravine," another impressive late novella about peasant life, tempers its realism with a strikingly allegorized plot, which may portend but doesn't excuse the infanticide Chekhov chooses for its gruesome climax.) On a single occasion Chekhov laid claim to the title that literary history grants him as if he were born with it— master of pathos. In "The Lady with the Pet Dog" Chekhov moves into the narrative with uninhibited sympathy for the weak and passionate lovers, and creates the most touching of all short stories about the weaknesses of men and women and the power of love. No story is less objective:

He went up to her and took her by the shoulders, to fondle her and say something diverting, and at that moment he caught sight of himself in the mirror.

His hair was already beginning to turn gray. And it seemed odd to him that he had grown so much older in the last few years, and lost his looks. The shoulders on which his hands rested were warm and heaving. He felt compassion for this life, still so warm and lovely, but probably about to begin to fade and wither like his own. Why did she love him so much? He always seemed to women different from what he was, and they loved in him not himself, but the man whom their imagination created and whom they had been eagerly seeking all their lives, and afterwards, when they saw their mistake, they loved him nevertheless. And not one of them had been happy with him. In the past he had met women, come together with them, parted from them, but he had never once loved; it was anything you please, but not love. And only now when his head was gray he had fallen in love, really, truly—for the first time in his life.

"The Lady with the Pet Dog" is not only great and affecting but a stunning *tour de force*: its shopworn dandy of a hero, if he were not saved in the nick of time by love (and, as he would insist, he really, truly is—the story is fragrant with the earthly salvation of its two poor souls), would find himself sooner or later in the grip of the horrors. Just once Chekhov wrote about the horrors, in his most autobiographical story, "The Black Monk." Because it is neither comic nor (except at the bitter end) pathetic, it is seldom reprinted; it isn't what Chekhov's readers expect now or expected then:

> My novella, "Three Years," will appear in the January issue of *Russian Thought*. The project was one thing but what resulted was something else, rather flabby and not silken as I wanted it to be but cambric. . . .
>
> I am fed up with the same thing all the time; I want to write about devils, about terrifying, volcanic women, about wizards—but alas! the demand is for well intentioned tales and stories from the life of the Ivan Gavriloviches and their spouses.

Chekhov is right about "Three Years," and might have said much the same thing even about a piece as fine and strong in its impulse, conception, and details as "My Life," another of his nearly novel-length stories that trace out the full trajectories of middle-class lives. Ultimately there is nothing surprising or inevitable about either. Short stories, as a species, tend to be more or less effective demonstrations of more or less complex and not too depressing theses about daily life (for which Chekhov's enthusiasm wasn't limitless: "So far as I can see, life is composed only of horrors, squabbles, and vulgarities, which either come in droves or follow one another"). Chekhov's stories aren't often exceptions to the rule, although, having written more stories than any other writer known to history, he could start up and set under way these little mechanisms more effortlessly than anybody else ever. But "The Black Monk" he must have written for himself, because it's about genius, the burden of consciousness, devils, and the bottomless pit. (Chekhov's favorite Russian writer wasn't Pushkin, with whom he is often compared for clarity and straightforwardness, but the grotesque fantasist Gogol.)

"The Black Monk" assembles evidence to prove that life is a bad dream from which some are lucky enough to awake into madness. In its details it's Chekhov's only unremitting allegory, an eerily mixed-up and hectic allegory of the fall, set in an Eden-like orchard supervised by a God-like old horticulturist with a marriageable daughter (could Chekhov have read "Rappaccini's Daughter"? but, except for the title character's materialization out of a whirlwind, "The Black Monk" has none of Hawthorne's Gothic claptrap). The hero is an urban intellectual, formerly the old man's ward, who returns to Eden for his nerves, regains his health, comes to reverence the old man, falls in love with the girl and marries her, and is about to live happily ever after when his wife discovers he is mad—. Complicated enough, but the story doesn't end here, and this summary omits mysterious "nasty" quarrels and reconciliations between father and daughter; the hero's yearning for "something gigantic, unfathomable, stupendous"; and the apparition of the black monk (insinuating *Doppelgänger*), who materializes to persuade the hero that intellectuals are "the chosen of God" and the vanguard of the millennial future. But Eve sees to it that Adam (and Samson! "his head was closely cropped, his beautiful long hair was gone") is cured of seeing things. So he learns to hate his wife and her father ("How fortunate Buddha, Mahomed, and Shakespeare were that their kind relations and doctors did not cure them of their ecstasy and their inspiration"):

> Before going to bed, Tanya said to him:
> "Father adores you. You are cross with him about something, and it is killing him. Look at him; he is ageing, not from day to day, but from hour to hour. I entreat you, Andryusha, for God's sake, for the sake of your dead father, for the sake of my peace of mind, be affectionate to him."

"I can't, I don't want to."

"But why?" asked Tanya, beginning to tremble all over. "Explain why."

"Because he is antipathetic to me, that's all," said Kovrin carelessly; and he shrugged his shoulders. "But we won't talk about him: he is your father."

"I can't understand, I can't," said Tanya, pressing her hands to her temples and staring at a fixed point. "Something incomprehensible, awful, is going on in the house. You have changed, grown unlike yourself. . . . You, clever, extraordinary man as you are, are irritated over trifles, meddle in paltry nonsense. . . . Such trivial things excite you, that sometimes one is simply amazed and can't believe that it is you. Come, come, don't be angry," she went on, kissing his hands, frightened of her own words. "You are clever, kind, noble. You will be just to father. He is so good."

"He is not good; he is just good-natured. Burlesque old uncles like your father, with well-fed, good-natured faces, extraordinarily hospitable and queer, at one time used to touch me and amuse me in novels and in farces and in life; now I dislike them. They are egoists to the marrow of their bones. What disgusts me most of all is their being so well-fed, and that purely bovine, purely hoggish optimism of a full stomach."

Tanya sat down on the bed and laid her head on the pillow.

"This is torture," she said, and from her voice it was evident that she was utterly exhausted, and that it was hard for her to speak.

"Not one moment of peace since the winter. . . . Why, it's awful! My God! I am wretched."

"Oh, of course, I am Herod, and you and your father are the innocents. Of course." [All ellipses Chekhov's.]

—and, forsaking Eve, he teaches her to hate him in return: "My father has just died. I owe that to you, for you have killed him. Our garden is being ruined; strangers are managing it already—that is, the very thing is happening that poor father dreaded. That, too, I owe to you. I hate you with my whole soul, and I hope you may soon perish." Happily, in the last moment of his life, as he collapses dying of a tubercular hemorrhage (his t.b., introduced a few pages before the end of this fifty-page story, is another perverse and cruel shock to the reader), the black monk appears to him again, restores his

madness, and allows him to die in a dream of Eve and the un-
fallen Eden:

> "Why did you not believe me?" he asked reproachfully,
> looking affectionately at Kovrin. "If you had believed me then,
> that you were a genius, you would not have spent these two
> years so gloomily and so wretchedly."
>
> Kovrin already believed that he was one of God's chosen
> and a genius; he vividly recalled his conversations with the
> monk in the past and tried to speak, but the blood flowed from
> his throat on to his breast, and not knowing what he was doing,
> he passed his hands over his breast, and his cuffs were soaked
> with blood. He tried to call Varvara Nikolaevna, who was
> asleep behind the screen; he made an effort and said:
>
> "Tanya!"
>
> He fell to the floor, and propping himself on his arms,
> called again:
>
> "Tanya!"
>
> He called Tanya, called to the great garden with the gor-
> geous flowers sprinkled with dew, called to the park, the pines
> with their shaggy roots, the rye-field, his marvellous learning,
> his youth, courage, joy—called to life, which was so lovely. He
> saw on the floor near his face a great pool of blood, and was too
> weak to utter a word, but an unspeakable, infinite happiness
> flooded his whole being. Below, under the balcony, they were
> playing the serenade, and the black monk whispered to him that
> he was a genius, and that he was dying only because his frail
> human body had lost its balance and could no longer serve as a
> mortal garb of genius.
>
> When Varvara Nikolaevna woke up and came out from
> behind the screen, Kovrin was dead, and a blissful smile was set
> upon his face.

Chekhov married Olga Knipper in 1901; he had three years to
live. (Potapenko, who had been out of touch, wrote him on a
literary matter, and Chekhov replied breaking the news: "I've
got married. But at my age this is no more worth mentioning
than growing bald.") Olga and Chekhov had been lovers, and
seem to have enjoyed each other's company when they could be
together. Mostly, though, Olga was living in Moscow, a leading actress at the Moscow Art Theater, and Chekhov was in
Yalta because of his illness; she wrote him anxious, pouting,

depressed, demanding, unreasonable, offended, grandiose, semi-hysterical letters (which must at least have stirred him up a bit), and he answered patiently, affectionately, wearily. Her letters after their first parting (it must be borne in mind that Olga was no child-bride—she was thirty-three and Chekhov forty-one at the time of their marriage) could scarcely have been more insensitive:

> "Anton, you must now write something new. There are so many subjects in your head. Don't be lazy, darling. Do make an effort to write." Four days later: "Anton, write something. I can hardly wait for the time when I shall read your new story. Write, darling. It will help to while away the time of our separation." Again three days later: "I am glad that you are writing, though only reluctantly. Work, darling, work." . . . "Darling, don't you feel any pleasure in being able to write? Doesn't it thrill you? . . . You are my great genius. You are the Russian Maupassant." And next day: "Don't give way to melancholy. Write something more for me and for Russia."[10]

—and so on, till she ends 1901 with New Year's greetings: "Darling Anton, are you going to start work or not? Please make a little effort. Surely your time will pass more quickly if you are writing. Don't you think so? I know you will write something nice, something elegant—elegant in form, of course. I feel terribly excited about it already." Meanwhile Chekhov, in Yalta, was hemorrhaging almost daily (as he apologetically let her know) and able to write no more than a few lines a day before being overcome by nervous and physical exhaustion.

Ivan Bunin tells of visiting them on one of Chekhov's rare occasions in Moscow after the marriage:

> . . . Olga, with a night off, elected to go to a charity concert with Nemirovich-Danchenko. Her escort, handsome in his tails and smelling of cigar smoke and eau de cologne, arrived, and Olga, young, fresh, and especially lovely in her evening dress, said to her husband: "Don't be bored without me, darling, but I know you're always happy with Bukishonchik. *Au revoir*, sweet"—and departed. Bunin was delighted to be allowed to

[10]Magarshack, pp. 361-362.

remain and chat with his friend. Chekhov washed his head while he reminisced about his past, his family, or discussed mutual literary acquaintances. Bunin also remembered that on this occasion Chekhov dreamed out loud, as he had done several times recently, of wanting to go off as a wanderer to holy places and then settle down in some monastery near a forest and lake where he could sit on a bench outside the gates on the long summer evenings. . . . At about four in the morning Olga returned, reeking of wine. "What, you are not yet asleep, darling? That's bad. And you are still here, Bukishonchik, but of course he's not bored with you!"[11]

Several months before his death, a silly literary woman with whom he had corresponded over the years sent him what she must have considered a Dostoevskian letter:

> I would very much like to see you, to speak to you in order to relieve my mind of much that is so hateful to me. It is all the more ludicrous and sad, especially at my age when life has passed, to carry on so painfully! Truly, it is shameful. In all conscience, however, I do not feel that I have deserved it. Forgive this unsolicited frankness, Anton Pavlovich. Although I did not seek it, I've seized this opportunity. I feared I would die without succeeding in saying that I have always profoundly esteemed you and regarded you as the best of men. And what of it if I have lowered myself in your opinion? So it had to be. It has been the greatest sorrow of my life. Now it is time to say it. . . . I don't want you to forgive me, but I do want you to understand.

—and Chekhov's reply closes the door firmly on all the literary agonies of the Russian nineteenth century:

> Forgive me. I'm frozen, for I've just returned from Tsaritsyno . . . my hands can hardly write and I must pack. All the best to you, keep cheerful, take a less complicated view of life, for it is probably much simpler in reality. And whether life, of which we know nothing, deserves all the tormenting thoughts on which our Russian minds wear themselves out—this is still a question.[12]

---

[11]Simmons, p. 618.

[12]Both letters are quoted from Simmons, pp. 621-622. Neither appears in Karlinsky or Yarmolinsky.

His death came quite suddenly in a hotel room in Germany, where he and Olga had gone for a vacation. ("What a despairing heap of boredom is this German resort Badenweiler!" he wrote to a friend.) One evening he improvised for her a comic story about hungry tourists. He fell asleep, but woke up at midnight and asked her to call a doctor (it was a request he had never made before). When the doctor entered the room, Chekhov raised his head and said in a decisive voice, *"Ich sterbe!"* (He made a point of seeing everything clearly to the very end.) The doctor had ordered champagne to ease Chekhov's breathing; Chekhov (in Olga's words) "picked up the glass, turned to me, smiled his wonderful smile and said: "It's been such a long time since I've had champagne.' He drank it all to the last drop, quietly lay down on his left side and was soon silent forever." "Even if Olga Knipper had invented all this," says Karlinsky, who quotes it, "there could hardly have been a more appropriate death scene for Chekhov, with its apt symbols for life, affirmation and stoic acceptance of the inevitable." But Chekhov, boyish charmer who knew all about upbeat or tart-and-tender endings, last mad genius of the great Russian century, might have demurred: "I am fed up with the same thing all the time; I want to write about devils, about terrifying, volcanic women, about wizards—but alas! the demand is for well-intentioned tales from the life of the Ivan Gavriloviches and their spouses."

XI.
Solzhenitsyn

Innocence was no excuse. "For several decades political arrests were distinguished in our country precisely by the fact that people were arrested who were guilty of nothing and were therefore unprepared to put up any resistance whatsoever. There was a general feeling of being destined for destruction, a sense of having nowhere to escape from the GPU-NKVD (which, incidentally, given our internal passport system, was quite accurate). . . ." *The Gulag Archipelago* is the first true history of a country that, fearing to seem unreal, abolished history:

> This submissiveness was also due to ignorance of the mechanics of epidemic arrests. By and large, the *Organs* had no profound reasons for their choice of whom to arrest and whom not to arrest. They merely had over-all assignments, quotas for a specific number of arrests. These quotas might be filled on an orderly basis or wholly arbitrarily. In 1937 a woman came to the reception room of the Novocherkassk NKVD to ask what she should do about the unfed unweaned infant of a neighbor who had been arrested. They said: "Sit down, we'll find out." She sat there for two hours—whereupon they took her and tossed her into a cell. They had a total plan which had to be fulfilled in a hurry, and there was no one available to send out into the city—and here was this woman already in their hands!

Gogolian comic machinery had come to life in Mother Russia a century after Gogol: "Everyone maintained a serious mien, but everyone understood it was a farce, above all the boys of the convoy, who were the simplest sort of fellows. At the Novosibirsk Transit Prison in 1945 they greeted the prisoners with a roll call based on *cases*. 'So and so! Article 58-1a, twenty-five years.' The chief of the convoy guard was curious: 'What did you get it for?' 'For nothing at all.' 'You're lying. *The sentence for nothing at all is ten years.*' " Those who blame Stalin and hope for the best are reminded by Solzhenitsyn that, within months after the October Revolution, the Bolshevik leaders had already laid the juridical foundations of Wonderland[1]: a judiciary subservient to the executive, which could alter or override or impose or indeed originate any judgment; the only police force in history that was "legally" empowered to investigate, arrest, interrogate, prosecute, try, convict, imprison, and put to death; the very model of a modern Prosecutor General poisoning the air at the earliest political trials, N. V. Krylenko, "organizer of the Department of Exceptional Courts of the People's Commissariat of Justice," who declared in open session as early as 1918 that "fine points of jurisprudence are unnecessary" because the concept of guilt is "an old bourgeois concept which has now been uprooted" and only "class expediency" counts (in accordance with the rules of farce, anybody sooner or later becomes *it*; and theoretician Krylenko eventually had the satisfaction of being tried, convicted, and shot as a "ferocious enemy of the people").

---

[1] "In 1919 . . . executions were carried out in Moscow, Petrograd, and other cities *on the basis of lists*—in other words, free people were simply arrested and executed immediately, and right and left those elements of the intelligentsia considered *close to the Cadets* [the bourgeois Constitutional Democratic Party] were raked into prison." When Gorky tried to intercede for some of the jailed intellectuals, Lenin was amused: "What a misfortune, just think about it! What injustice!" and advised him "not to waste your energy whimpering over rotten intellectuals." *Five years* after the Revolution, revising the draft of a new Criminal Code, Lenin stressed the need for an institutionalization of terror, and added six articles specifying execution by shooting (one of them, for "propaganda and agitation") to the six proposed in the draft.

Well, then, were the "bluecaps" (the functionaries of Soviet State Security, whatever infamous cluster of initials they happened to be carrying at the moment; but changing their initials didn't help) as bad as the Gestapo? Worse, replies Solzhenitsyn:

> There is no way of sidestepping this comparison: both the years and the methods coincide too closely. And the comparison occurred even more naturally to those who had passed through the hands of both the Gestapo and the MGB. One of these was Yevgeny Ivanovich Divnich, an émigré and preacher of Orthodox Christianity. The Gestapo accused him of Communist activities among Russian workers in Germany, and the MGB charged him with having ties to the international bourgeoisie. Divnich's verdict was unfavorable to the MGB. He was tortured by both, but the Gestapo was nonetheless trying to get at the truth, and when the accusation did not hold up, Divnich was released. The MGB wasn't interested in the truth and had no intention of letting anyone out of its grip once he was arrested.

Comparisons between Nazi Germany and Soviet Russia don't sit well with certain intellectuals (not Lenin's "rotten" kind?), among them George Steiner, who has been specializing for years in the moral sensibility of the universe (on one occasion it took him five or six thousand words to pull himself together when some insensitive clod told him that commandants of Nazi death camps had been known to relax after a hot day at the ovens by reading Goethe and playing Schubert). "To infer that the Soviet terror is as hideous as Hitlerism is not only a brutal oversimplification but a moral indecency [why?]. Set out by themselves, the facts have no real meaning [why not?]"; and as for Divnich's first-hand testimony: "left bare, devoid of a moral and historical context as problematic as any human sensibility has ever had to face [not to mention the unproblematic torments and terrors that Solzhenitsyn and the millions of others had to face for ten and twenty years], these facts tend to a gross inference that the Gestapo was using torture merely to seek 'the truth.' "[2] Gross inferences from gross

---

[2]*The New Yorker*, August 5, 1974, pp. 83-4.

sensibilities. Steiner is a man of ideas and inferences (an intellectual no doubt); but Solzhenitsyn is interested in facts, what the beast actually did—beating, starving, piling together till the point of mass suffocation, confinement in the freezing cell or hot box, stamping on the genitals—and how often and where and when and to whom and how many. In the footnote on Divnich he offers important evidence about two different attitudes toward "truth," and he is so outraged by the *fact* of the MGB's worse-than-Nazi shamelessness as to ignore this opportunity to draw from the fact an important moral and historical inference: that the Nazis had boundaries (the Gestapo was the plug-ugly at the gate) while the Soviets had only goblins and alarms (the MGB was the maniac in the parlor); that it was possible to be a Nazi in Nazi Germany but impossible to be a Communist in Communist Russia; that a German who professed the right combination of loyalties and beliefs was and remained as acceptable a Nazi as any other, whereas a Russian couldn't profess *or fail to profess* anything whatever that mightn't sooner or later be used against him. The Nazis had a community, with articles of agreement and exclusion. The Soviets had the innumerable estranging "islands" of the Archipelago—death for a word and ten years for nothing at all—to instruct their people that, because the system was by moral and economic definition perfect, its failure to work perfectly was the criminal responsibility of a whole population of slackers, wreckers, traitors, rotten intellectuals. If the Western political dilettante would like to think that Stalin (the maniac in the attic) or certainly Lenin or at least Trotsky was "better" than Hitler—at any rate that the Soviet polity is susceptible of moral amelioration and the Nazi was not—Solzhenitsyn says nothing to contradict him. The author of *The Gulag Archipelago* isn't a Fascist, and he's as immoderate and exacerbated a Russian patriot as Dostoevsky; but he's writing history,[3] not prophecy.

---

[3]*Current* history, according to *American P.E.N. Newsletter* #15 (Summer 1974):

> American P.E.N. has protested the alleged torture of USSR writer Valentin Moroz. In a telegram sent to N. V. Podgorny, President of the USSR, the Center wrote: "American P.E.N.

Because he works with facts, Solzhenitsyn isn't sentimental about the Old Bolsheviks as, puzzling over the "riddle" of the show trials, men of ideas and inferences are inclined to be: he isn't, for instance, surprised to find Bukharin—the leading Party theoretician, "the favorite of the Party" (in the words of Lenin's Testament), last of the surviving front-rank Bolsheviks in Russia (Trotsky hadn't yet been assassinated in Mexico) except for Stalin—assuring Stalin in 1937 that everything the Great Leader has seen fit to do (including the millions of murders) has been proper and necessary. Bukharin was pleading for his life, and at the same time persuading himself that he was helping to preserve the *idea* of the Revolution; most of the others would have had similar feelings; and they ended as they did because they were weak, conceited, frightened, used-up men who had had relatively easy lives even during their short stints in Tsarist exile or prisons (which by the evidence Solzhenitsyn presents must have been rather like American minimum-security facilities for embezzlers and careless politicians). For years they must have been hearing the news about large-scale corrective methods introduced and perfected by their old comrade the Great Cannibal, and their hearts failed them:

> . . . where is the riddle? How they were *worked over*? Very simply: Do you want to *live*? (And even those who don't care about themselves care about their children or grandchildren.) Do you understand that it takes absolutely no effort to have you shot, without your ever leaving the courtyards of the GPU? (And there was no doubt whatever about that. Whoever hadn't yet

---

deeply concerned by reports that Valentin Moroz subject to extreme and continuous torture in Vladimir Prison, beatings, poisoning, arranged brutality by armed criminal sadists in an effort to force him to recant his opinions. . . ."

American P.E.N. has also communicated its sorrow at the sentence imposed on Gabriel Superfin after his trial in Orel, May 12-14. Superfin, a 30-year-old Moscow literary critic who claimed he was not allowed legal counsel, was given five years confinement in a strict regime labor camp and two years exile for his purported anti-Soviet activities. Before his trial Superfin had been held in solitary confinement for eight months.

Superfin was credited by Solzhenitsyn for help in collecting materials for *August 1914*.

learned it would be given a course in being ground down by the Lubyanka.) But it is useful both for you and for us to have you act out a certain drama . . . you'll see that no one who behaved has been shot. . . . But the understanding is that you have to carry out *all* our conditions to the very last! The trial must work for the good of socialist society.

(Those who wouldn't make a deal committed suicide or were tortured to death or shot.) Still, the details of the long, slow, lazy cat-and-mouse game Stalin played with Bukharin are fascinating, Bukharin abject and hoping against hope ("Dear Koba! Dear Koba!"—"Koba" was Stalin's nickname in the early Party days, when he robbed banks for the Party), Stalin courteous and playful ("Come on, now! No one is going to expel you from the Party!"):

> Bukharin believed him and revived. He willingly assured the Plenum of his repentance, and immediately abandoned his hunger strike. (At home he said: "Come on now, cut me some sausage! Koba said they wouldn't expel me.") But in the course of the Plenum, Kaganovich and Molotov (impudent fellows they were, indeed!—paid no attention to Stalin's opinion!) both called Bukharin a Fascist hireling and demanded that he be shot.[4]

But Stalin's feline intricacies weren't yet exhausted. As cream of the jest, he would have the mouse—great theoretician!—create a beautiful Constitution; and "Bukharin wrote every last word of our entire existing—in other words, nonexis-

---

[4]Solzhenitsyn adds a footnote: "See what a wealth of information we are deprived of because we're protecting Molotov's noble old age." (Earlier: "symbol of them all, the smug and stupid Molotov lives on at Granovsky No. 3, a man who has learned nothing at all, even now, though he is saturated with our blood and nobly crosses the sidewalk to seat himself in his long, wide automobile.") Solzhenitsyn has some grim fun with footnotes, especially when he wishes to remind his compatriots that the assassins are still larking along without a worry in the world if they haven't died in tranquil old age: "Today Lozovsky [provocateur and stool pigeon] holds the degree of candidate in medical sciences and lives in Moscow. Everything is going well with him"; "Viktor Andreyevich Seryegin [formerly a political commissar in the army and of course an energetic accomplice in frameups] lives in Moscow today and works in a Consumer Service Combine attached to the Moscow Soviet. He lives well."

tent—Constitution, which is so beautiful to listen to." Shortly before Bukharin's trial, the document was adopted "with fanfare and celebration and named . . . the Stalinist Constitution for all eternity." The ultimate irony—which Solzhenitsyn, requiring Stalin's villainy to be without a flaw even in the grave, doesn't acknowledge—is that the public protests which a handful of Soviet citizens have been making in recent years against their government justify themselves on the authority of this Constitution (because Orwell was wrong and Newspeak never really happens: love means love, peace means peace, and Stalin in the grave is undercut by Bukharin's words as Hitler could never be by Goebbels's or his own; socialism, like the Church, is stuck with a lovely vocabulary; a document which is beautiful to listen to has beautiful meanings which are always understood and will sooner or later be acted on by *some*body).

How shudderingly Solzhenitsyn loathes the dead image of Stalin! the supreme villain! and yet needs to insist on seeing in him only vanity, stupidity, mediocrity. The schizophrenia explodes with a dull thud in the chapter in which Solzhenitsyn, denouncing capital punishment, cries out abruptly: "Even if Stalin had killed no others, I believe he deserved to be drawn and quartered just for the lives of those six Tsarskoye Selo peasants!" Solzhenitsyn asks, "Where is the riddle?" But his inescapable riddle is Stalin, who for nearly three decades kept an immense country in paralysis and waking nightmare by the force of example, precedent, Marxist or pseudo-Marxist doctrine, party discipline, police terror, patriotic war—but mostly, it seems, by the force of that vain, stupid, mediocre personality. All the irony, sarcasm, anger, indignation, rage, fury that drive Solzhenitsyn through this chronicle of wasted time beat themselves raw against the sense of waste, loss, imbecile repetition, monotony, immobility. The same gray tableau: Stalin in the doorway watching impassively, the victim spreadeagled on his back held by four guards while the prison boss prepares to take what he calls his "penalty kick," the masses turned away from the scene with their noses buried in *Pravda* ("Truth") or *Izvestiya* ("News"), none of them capable of deviating an inch from his appointed posture. So when Solzhenitsyn comes across a live one, the book and the reader get a lift that momentarily fetches them straight up out of the chamber of horrors and into the regions of light.

In 1937 the Stalin apparatus was organizing show trials out in the provinces for the purpose of exposing to the masses "the black soul of the opposition." As one of the defendants it picked Vasily Grigoryevich Vlasov, head of the District Consumer Cooperative of the village of Kady in remote Ivanovo Province. He had already angered the District Prosecutor by refusing him special favors and the NKVD by protecting two of his subordinates against charges of "wrecking." When an honest official was slandered, Vlasov called for the slanderer's expulsion from the Party; but the slandered man was arrested and, after he had been tortured to death, a full confession was published over his name. The slanderer became district head of the Party. The Deputy Chairman of the district NKVD came to Vlasov with "a peace proposal"—in return for a small bribe, Vlasov's safety would be guaranteed—and Vlasov threw him out. Thereupon Vlasov was requested to bring charges at a Party meeting against two of the local administrators, so that the NKVD could trap him by asking why he hadn't informed on them earlier! Vlasov refused: "I won't make the report! Let Krylov make the report—after all, he arrested Smirnov and Univer and is handling their case." Krylov: "I'm not familiar with the evidence." Vlasov: "If even *you* aren't familiar with the evidence, that means they were arrested without cause." And Solzhenitsyn comments: "So the Party meeting simply didn't take place. But how often did people dare to defend themselves?" Vlasov's friends collected money for him and begged him to run away; but he refused. The district newspaper began attacking the Consumer Cooperative. Meanwhile Vlasov had managed to work out an ingeniously practical way of (1) complying with government directives intended to deprive the people of bread, and (2) having large quantities of bread baked locally and distributed to the local inhabitants, who (3) hitherto had had to travel long distances and wait in long lines for the centralized and inadequate government distribution. At last he was arrested and "charged with: (1) initiating bread lines; (2)

having an inadequate minimum assortment of merchandise
. . . ; (3) procuring a surplus of salt." Klyugin, NKVD trial
manager, came to Vlasov's cell: "You've got to admit your
guilt and tell the whole truth!" Vlasov: "The truth and nothing
but the truth, . . . that you are every bit as bad as the German
Fascists!" Klyugin: "Listen here, you whore, you'll pay with
your blood!"[5] When Saburov, another defendant, "begged
that his life be spared—'not for me, but for my little children'—
Vlasov, out of vexation, pulled him back by the jacket: 'You're
a fool.' " In his last statement to the court Vlasov said: "I
consider you not a court but actors pretending to be a court in a
stage farce where roles have already been written for you.
You are engaged in a repulsive provocation on the part of the
NKVD. You are going to sentence me to be shot no matter
what I say. I believe one thing only: the time will come when
you will be here in my place." (Solzhenitsyn's regretful footnote reveals that this final prediction was inaccurate.) Later
the verdict was read:

> After the solemn words "To be shot!" the judges paused
> for applause. But the mood in the hall was so gloomy . . . that
> no applause was to be heard even from the first two benches,
> where the Party members were sitting. This, indeed, was totally
> improper. "Oh, good Lord, what have you done?" someone in
> the hall shouted at the members of the court. Univer's wife dis-
> solved in tears. In the half-darkness, the crowd began to stir.
> Vlasov shouted at the front benches:
> "Come on, you bastards, why aren't you clapping? Some
> Communists you are!"
> The political commissar of the guards platoon ran up to
> him and shoved his revolver in his face. Vlasov reached out to
> grab the revolver, but a policeman ran up and pushed back his
> political commissar, who had been guilty of a blunder. The chief
> of the convoy gave the command: "Arms at the ready!" And
> thirty police carbines and the pistols of the local NKVD men
> were aimed at the defendants and at the crowd. . . .

---

[5]Solzhenitsyn's footnote: "Your own blood, too, is going to flow soon, Klyugin! Caught in the Yezhov gang of gaybisty [secret police], Klyugin will have
his throat cut by the stool pigeon Gubaidulin."

Soon after, the apparatus decided that political trials would be private in the future (Vlasov's trial, altogether too public, had been reported in the provincial newspapers). What was the world coming to, when a defendant was so unsophisticated he couldn't be managed? Bukharin and the other old pros knew their place, but Stalin was fresh out of old pros.

A man like Vlasov is too extravagant for fiction,[6] his adventures have to be matters of fact. By comparison with such volcanic eruptions of fact, Solzhenitsyn's books of fiction seem cautious, sluggish, "objective," "universal" (partly, no doubt, because the novelist feared that close particularity might increase the risk of police reprisal against his informanists): Nobel-Prize fiction, testifying to the persistence of hope, the possibility of love and justice, the validity of suffering as chapter by chapter we all lurch meritoriously through the parched desert of fictional psychologizing ("Lavrenty Pavlovich was one of those young men who . . ."). *Ivan Denisovich* is an earnest quasi-documentary; the portrait of Stalin in *The First Circle* is effective in a restrained and long-winded mode (*Gulag* and history can do it with a stroke: "The OSO . . . was subordinate only to the Minister of Internal Affairs, to Stalin, and to Satan"), but nothing cheerful in the novel goes much beyond the female tractor-driver school of socialist realism; *The Cancer Ward* is medical soap-opera.[7] *August 1914*, on the other hand, is an ex-

---

[6]And for history! Incredibly, he survived (most of his co-defendants were shot before they reached the death calls, because the prison they were sent to was already overcrowded), making a "nineteen-year-long journey through the Archipelago." Vlasov waited forty-one days for execution (with fourteen other prisoners in a cell "intended for solitary confinement, sixteen feet long and a little more than three feet wide"), he spat in the face of the district Chief of the Investigation Department who for some undisclosed reason had come to see him, and he refused the suggestion of his jailers that he petition to be pardoned. "But on the forty-second day they . . . informed him that the Presidium of the Supreme Soviet had commuted the supreme measure of punishment to twenty years of imprisonment in corrective-labor camps with disenfranchisement for five additional years."

[7]Solzhenenitsyn the writer of fiction is almost as limited to poster-type emotions as any Writers-Union hack. But now and then the novels reveal, however discreetly, his fondness for women and sex: it's their only endearing personal touch; and, since tyranny (modern tyranny at any rate) is inseparable from artistic prudery, it's also their only artistic triumph over tyranny.

pert piece of *technical* writing, interesting (if also fatiguing) for Solzhenitsyn's relentless spelling out of military detail, as well as for the relentless, occasionally apoplectic partisanship with which he attributes the Russian army's defeats to "wooden-headed" and cowardly generals (a mere inversion of Tolstoy's populist theorizing about war, which Solzhenitsyn mocks at and dismisses in the book). *August 1914* is the first installment of a series intended to be almost or mainly history; but, like the earlier novels, it is preliminary to Solzhenitsyn's important work—which he begins with *The Gulag Archipelago* (police seizure of the ms. having settled the question of risk to his informants)—as the first inside historian of the débâcle of twentieth-century Russia:

> And how we burned in the camps later, thinking: What would things have been like if every Security operative, when he went out at night to make an arrest, had been uncertain whether he would return alive and had to say good-bye to his family? Or if, during periods of mass arrests, as for example in Leningrad, when they arrested a quarter of the entire city, people had not simply sat there in their lairs, paling with terror at every bang of the downstairs door and at every step on the staircase, but had understood they had nothing left to lose and had boldly set up in the downstairs hall an ambush of half dozen people with axes, hammers, pokers, or whatever else was at hand? After all, you knew ahead of time that those bluecaps were out at night for no good purpose. And you could be sure ahead of time that you'd be cracking the skull of a cutthroat. Or what about the Black Maria sitting out there on the street with one lonely chauffeur—what if it had been driven off or its tires spiked? The Organs would very shortly have suffered a shortage of officers and transport and, notwithstanding all of Stalin's thirst, the cursed machine would have ground to a halt!

But nobody (except Vlasov) made a move, and the farce went on: "The machine stamped out the sentences. The prisoner had already been deprived of all rights when they cut off his buttons on the threshold of State Security, and he couldn't avoid a stretch. The members of the legal profession were so used to this that they fell on their faces in 1958 and caused a big scandal. The text of the projected new 'Fundamental Principles of

Criminal Prosecution of the U.S.S.R.' was published in the newspapers, and they'd *forgotten* to include any reference to *possible* grounds for acquittal. The government newspaper issued a mild rebuke: '*The impression might be created* that our courts only bring in convictions.' " The typewriters continued to type out dossiers, neither the physical presence nor even a photo of the prisoner was necessary, the speed of the verdicts "was limited only by the technology of typewriting"; and how could The Great Typewriter have guessed that there was more to a prisoner named Solzhenitsyn than his dossier?

Acknowledgments

For their permission to reprint parts of this book originally published by them, I am grateful to the Oxford University Press and the Cambridge University Press; and especially to *The Hudson Review*, in which all but two of the foregoing chapters first appeared.